KT-592-674

PROJECT MANAGEMENT

A Harvard Business Review Paperback

Harvard Business Review paperback No. 90053

The *Harvard Business Review* articles in this collection
are available individually. Discounts apply to quantity
purchases. For information and ordering, contact Operations Department, Harvard Business School Publishing
Division, Boston, MA 02163. Telephone: (617) 495-6192.
Fax: (617) 495-6985.

© 1959, 1985, 1986, 1987, 1989, 1991 by the President and
Fellows of Harvard College.

Editor's Note: Some articles included in this book may have
been written before authors and editors began to take into
consideration the role of women in management. We hope
the archaic usage representing all managers as male does not
detract from the usefulness of the collection.

All rights reserved. No part of this book may be reproduced,
stored in a retrieval system, or transmitted, in any form or by
any means, electronic, mechanical, photocopying, recording,
or otherwise without the prior written permission of the
copyright holder.
Printed in the United States of America.
93 92 91   5 4 3 2 1

Contents

Evaluation

Must Finance and Strategy Clash?
Patrick Barwise, Paul R. Marsh, and Robin Wensley
3

Marketing and finance often disagree about long-term strategic investments. When project analysis is done correctly, however, an investment that makes good marketing sense will also provide competitive advantage.

Pitfalls in Evaluating Risky Projects
James E. Hodder and Henry E. Riggs
9

Are discounted cash flow techniques biased against investments in new programs and projects? Not if they avoid certain simplistic assumptions.

Assessing Capital Risk: You Can't Be Too Conservative
Jasper H. Arnold III
17

A worst case forecast is usually too good. Staying power analysis is a better way to look at the downside of a project or program.

Implementation

The Project Manager
Paul O. Gaddis
29

First published in 1959, this article has become the classic definition of the project manager.

How to Make a Team Work
Maurice Hardaker and Bryan K. Ward
39

A management team can unwittingly push a project down several different paths. The IBM solution is to get the key players to start off facing in the same direction.

You *Can* Manage Construction Risks
John D. Macomber
45

Construction is old technology, but it can be disastrously expensive if it is managed poorly. A seven-step protocol can help you analyze and control construction risk.

Knowing When to Pull the Plug
Barry M. Staw and Jerry Ross
57

A manager can deny, against clear evidence, that a project is doomed. At a certain point pulling the plug is in everyone's best interest.

Post-Project Appraisals Pay
Frank R. Gulliver
65

Evaluating a completed project is an opportunity for learning fundamental lessons about a business. The larger the project and investment, the more valuable the lessons will be.

Evaluation

*Marketing and finance are complementary
– when the analysis is right.*

Must Finance and Strategy Clash?

by Patrick Barwise, Paul R. Marsh, and Robin Wensley

Marketers and finance people seldom see eye to eye. The marketers say, "This product will open up a whole new market segment." Finance people respond, "It's a bad investment. The IRR is only 8%." Why are they so often in opposition?

The financial criteria used to decide if a project will be profitable are entirely consistent with the tenets of competitive marketing analysis. Correctly applied, good financial analysis complements rather than contradicts good marketing analysis. In practice, though, the analysis usually falls short. That explains why a strategic investment's projected returns are so often out of line with the marketing and strategic logic.

From a financial perspective, a good investment is one with a positive net present value – that is, one whose value exceeds its costs. While marketers often think a project's NPV is merely the result of financial arithmetic, in reality, it is derived from strategic marketing issues. To have a positive NPV, a project must pass two tests[1]: Does the product or service have enough value to enough customers to support prices and volumes that exceed the costs of supplying it – including the opportunity cost of capital? This question is central to postwar marketing and the "marketing concept." Second, does the company have enough sources of sustainable competitive advantage to exploit, develop, and defend the opportunity? This reflects marketing's more recent emphasis

on competitive strategy. The trick, then, is to encourage an investment decision-making process in which the financial analysis highlights rather than masks these two fundamental marketing questions.

Consider Fashion Bathrooms, a disguised but real division of a diversified engineering company that makes traditional cast-iron bathtubs. The CEO and her senior managers were considering new investments. One option was to adopt a novel proprietary casting process to make lighter bathtubs that could compete better against plastic ones. The $20 million investment seemed wise from a marketing perspective, but the investment's NPV came to a negative $2 million.

> Good analysis ties the details of strategy to the financial implications.

A debate ensued. Some top managers put their faith in the numbers. They believed that although the project would produce a superior product in many respects, its capital requirements were excessive. To the CEO and some others, however, Project

1. Patrick Barwise, Paul Marsh, and Robin Wensley, "Strategic Investment Decisions," *Research in Marketing,* vol. 9, 1987, pp. 1-57.

Patrick Barwise is senior lecturer in marketing, and Paul R. Marsh is deputy principal, faculty dean, and professor of management and finance – both at London Business School. Robin Wensley is chairman of Warwick Business School, where he teaches strategic marketing.

Lightweight still made intuitive sense. They wanted to go ahead with it despite the negative returns. As the marketing director put it, "There are some investments you have to make simply to stay in business – regardless of their rate of return."

In the end, what was good for Fashion Bathrooms in a marketing sense was also good for it financially. The initial analysis simply failed to reflect that reality. To sharpen the financial analysis, the managers returned to the marketing strategy and delved deeper into it. Now the financial analysis helped clarify the marketing issues to be reconsidered.

Good project evaluation considers *all* the relevant factors, including hard-to-quantify costs and benefits. It also takes into account the more neglected consequences of *not* investing. It recognizes the value of opening up options and, by not arbitrarily restricting the time horizon or setting discount rates too high, avoids undervaluing long-term projects. Understanding project evaluation is easy. Doing it is the real challenge.

Use the Right Base Case

Finance theory assumes that a project will be evaluated against its base case, that is, what will happen if the project is not carried out. Managers tend to explore fully the implications of adopting the project but usually spend less time considering the likely outcome of not making the investment. Yet unless the base case is realistic, the incremental cash flows – the difference between the "with" and the "without" scenarios – will mislead.

Often companies implicitly assume that the base case is simply a continuation of the status quo, but this assumption ignores market trends and competitor behavior. It also neglects the impact of changes the company might make anyway, like improving operations management.

Using the wrong base case is typical of product launches in which the new product will likely erode the market for the company's existing product line. Take Apple Computer's introduction of the Macintosh SE. The new PC had obvious implications for sales of earlier generation Macintoshes. To analyze the incremental cash flows arising from the new product, Apple would have needed to count the lost contribution from sales of its existing products as a cost of the launch.

Wrongly applied, however, this approach would equate the without case to the status quo: it would assume that without the SE, sales of existing Macintoshes would continue at their current level. In the competitive PC market, however, nothing stands still. Competitors like IBM would likely innovate and take share away from the earlier generation Macintoshes – which a more realistic base case would have reflected. Sales of existing products would decline even in the base case.

Consider investments in the marketing of existing brands through promotions, media budgets, and the like. They are often sold as if they were likely to lead to ever-increasing market share. But competitors will also be promoting their brands, and market shares across the board still have to add up to 100%. Still, such an investment is not necessarily wasted. It may just need a more realistic justification: although the investment is unlikely to increase sales above existing levels, it may prevent sales from falling. Marketers who like positive thinking may not like this defensive argument, but it is the only argument that makes economic sense in a mature market.

In situations like this, when the investment is needed just to maintain market share, the returns may be high in comparison with the base case, but the company's reported profits may still go down. Senior managers are naturally puzzled at apparently netting only 5% on a project that had promised a 35% return.[2] Without the investment, however, the profit picture would have looked even worse, especially in the longer term.

Some projects disappoint for other reasons. Sometimes the original proposals are overoptimistic, partly because the base case is implicit or defined incorrectly. That is, if managers are convinced that the investment is sound and are frustrated because the figures fail to confirm their intuition, they may overinflate projections of sales or earnings. But misstating the base case and then having to make unrealistic projections are unlikely to cancel each other out; they merely cloud the analysis.

The base case against which Fashion Bathrooms first compared Project Lightweight implicitly assumed that sales would stay the same without the investment. In fact, sales were declining. When managers reevaluated the project using the correct base case, the negative NPV disappeared. The finance director also began to question the discount rate. He had at first used a high rate because the volumes and therefore the cost savings seemed very uncertain. At the time, Fashion Bathrooms had two plants, both running below capacity. Project Lightweight would upgrade one, so only products made at that plant would benefit from the new efficiencies. The finance director realized, however, that Fashion Bathrooms could shift all production to the upgraded plant until

2. Joseph L. Bower, *Managing the Resource Allocation Process* (Boston: Harvard Business School Press, 1986), p.13.

it hit full capacity. That way, the company would be sure to get the full savings. The second plant would handle only the overflow.

Other managers at Fashion Bathrooms thought that exiting the business was a more relevant base case. This alternative proved to be unattractive. The company would face heavy closure costs, and its plants had few alternative uses and therefore very low resale value.

Define the Project Boundaries

Advising managers to get the base case right is like telling them to get the project right. Obviously, the advice is grossly simplistic. One difficult task, for instance, is defining the project's boundaries: What is the correct without case – exiting the business, carrying on as things are now, improving distribution and marketing? And what is the right version of the project? Usually, there are several quite different ways of implementing it.

The project's boundaries tend to shift during the course of the analysis. Different players view the investment differently. For the CEO of Fashion Bathrooms, the without case was the dismal prospect of soldiering on in a declining market, while the investment was a way to improve morale and signal a commitment to stay in business. The manager of the plant that would not be upgraded saw things differently. While the without case would allow his factory to maintain its production level, the with case was a sure route to reduced output and diminished personal status – or even the loss of his job.

In principle, managers should take a corporate perspective when considering incremental costs and benefits. In practice, this is unrealistic. Unit managers' own responsibilities and self-interest will influence their perception of the project and color the way they define and analyze the proposal.

A project may look good at the business unit level because it shifts costs or steals share from another unit. From the corporate perspective, such a project would be less appealing. Fashion Bathrooms' parent company had a minimal share of the plastic bathtub market, so management ignored any erosion that Project Lightweight might cause. Had the plastics division been larger or more important, corporate management would have wanted the analysis to include the loss for the plastics division as well as the gain for the cast-iron bathtub division.

One might expect the boundaries of a project to be defined more broadly at the corporate level than at the business unit level. This is not always the case.

"Hey, what a great desk! I almost wish I were a scribe, instead of a Pharisee."

The CEO of Fashion Bathrooms, for instance, proposed the ambitious idea of combining marketing for the plastic and cast-iron divisions. The parent company board discouraged her from pursuing this course. It wanted her to narrow her focus and first sort out the operating and marketing problems at Fashion Bathrooms.

Choose an Appropriate Time Horizon

Project boundaries are also defined in terms of time. A project's financial analysis often extends over whichever is shorter: the assets' physical economic life or some arbitrary time horizon, like ten years. In the final year, the analysis may include minimal salvage values for the largest tangible assets. But financial appraisals seldom explain why a particular time horizon was chosen, even when the numbers are sensitive to the project's assumed life.

Strategic projects seldom have short or even easily defined lives. A plant built to manufacture a new branded product will eventually have to be replaced, but the product's value to the company, if successful, may easily outlast the plant. Or the plant's replacement date may extend beyond the time horizon used to appraise the project. None of this matters as long as the financial appraisal includes full economic terminal value rather than salvage amounts. The terminal value should reflect the cash flows over the remaining life of the existing plant or the value of the brand when the plant is replaced.

Some managers argue that it is pointless to look beyond ten years since cash flows will have only a small present value when discounted and since no one can accurately forecast that far ahead. But if terminal values are large, as they are for many strategic investments, they will be significant even when discounted. And that such values are notoriously hard to forecast is little reason to ignore them. Many strategic investments are designed to build a market position, a research capability, a reputation, or a brand name. Assuming that these assets are worthless beyond some arbitrary horizon fails to reflect the strategic reality.

The bathtub managers were fully aware that they had chosen an arbitrary time horizon for evaluating Project Lightweight. Their choice of ten years was purely pragmatic: there were ten columns on the company's capital-budgeting appraisal form. Since ten years was also the standard life over which plant and machinery were depreciated, they inserted no terminal value for the upgraded plant. In reality, however, the upgraded plant would last longer than ten years, and the market for cast-iron bathtubs was projected to continue well into the future.

Evaluate Options

Strategic investments usually go beyond exploitation of a particular opportunity. They open up options that extend even further into the future than the original project. When, for instance, Nestlé was considering its takeover of Rowntree, it paid close attention to the intangible assets. Nestlé was particularly interested in Rowntree's brands because of the marketing and distribution options they provided, especially in Europe in the run up to 1992.

Obviously, options stemming from investments in R&D, know-how, brand names, test markets, and channel developments have value beyond the initial investment. Less obvious is the value of the options to create subsequent products that complement or are based on existing ones.

Financial theorists and professionals have long been interested in valuing financial options like puts

and calls, warrants, and convertible bonds; valuation models for these options are well-known. More recently, however, theorists and practitioners have acknowledged the importance of options on real assets.[3] But quantitative models for valuing these kinds of options are almost impossible to apply in

A product brand may outlast the factory. Do you give it a terminal value?

practice, since truly strategic options are so vague and often depend on a manager's vision of what might happen.

Financial appraisals of strategic investments therefore usually focus on the opportunity at hand and seldom try to value market opportunities that the investment may create. Businesspeople try to compensate for this when it comes to making the real decision. As Richard A. Brealey and Stewart C. Myers wrote, "Businesspeople often act smarter than they talk....They may make correct decisions, but they may not be able to explain them in the language of finance."[4]

Fashion Bathrooms was well aware of the options that Project Lightweight could open for its cast-iron bathtub business. First was the possibility of modernizing the company's second plant by introducing the casting process there as well. The attractiveness of this action would depend on the success of the company in reversing the market decline. Second, Fashion Bathrooms could use the same brand name to produce complementary products like washbasins and shower trays. The company made no attempt to value these opportunities, partly because they were just ideas with a small chance of being implemented and partly because Project Lightweight already appeared financially worthwhile.

Unbundle the Costs and Benefits

Almost any strategic investment can be regarded as a bundle of component subprojects, each with different costs and benefits. It is useful to recognize this and unbundle the subprojects. Doing so simplifies the analysis and helps managers make forecasts and assumptions explicit. It may also help the proposers come up with a better alternative.

Take an investment in a highly competitive market, like a Main Street retailing operation. The investment is a combination of two things: an in-

3. See Stewart C. Myers, "Finance Theory and Financial Strategy," *Interfaces*, January-February 1984, pp. 126-137.

4. *Principles of Corporate Finance*, 3rd edition (New York: McGraw-Hill, 1988), p. 258.

5. Paul R. Marsh, Patrick Barwise, Kathryn Thomas, and Robin Wensley, "Managing Strategic Investment Decisions," in *Competitiveness and the Management Process*, ed. Andrew Pettigrew (Oxford: Basil Blackwell, 1988).

vestment in real estate and an investment in retailing skills. Yet financial evaluations normally lump these together, showing the total project as an initial investment in real estate plus shop-fitting costs, a stream of retailing profits, and a terminal value for the real estate and retailing business. A common problem with this formulation is that an over-optimistic terminal value for the real estate can make a bad retailing investment look good; a pessimistic value can make an efficient retailing operation look like a loser.

An alternative analysis would view the investment as two related projects. The first is a straight real estate investment, which includes the initial cost, a stream of rental receipts, and a terminal value. The second is a retailing investment, which involves the initial shop-fitting costs, the stream of retailing profits net of the rental, and the terminal value of the retailing operation.

Unless the company has a genuine competitive advantage in real estate, the NPV of the investment in real estate in the highly competitive Main Street market will probably be zero. Using the assumption of a zero NPV and given the purchase price and market rentals, managers can find the terminal value of the property. This shifts the focus to the second project, where the company may indeed have a competitive advantage. By stripping out the initial cost and the terminal values of the real estate and replacing these with the market rental, that is, with the opportunity cost of renting the space to another tenant, the company can evaluate the pure retailing project without the bias of an optimistic or pessimistic assumption about future real estate prices.

Performing the analysis this way clarifies the investment decision and avoids misleading forecasts. It also raises questions that might otherwise go unasked. In the Main Street deal, for example, it raises questions like: Would it be better to rent rather than buy the real estate? Or is it better to forgo the retailing project and invest in the real estate only?

Many strategic investments come packaged with investments in highly competitive and risky markets: overseas investments in manufacturing facilities may come with investments in foreign currency, investments in natural resource extraction may come with an investment in the resource itself, and so on. The best approach is to separate the investments in which the company has some competitive advantage from those in a highly competitive market and for which the NPV is likely to be zero.

Projects are also often bundled for political reasons. Proposers may include under the project umbrella a smaller project that would be hard to justify by itself. In one packaged-goods company, the executives buried in a large cost-saving investment a staff and office space upgrade and an investment in a new computer system. Although related to the cost-saving project, these additions were not essential to it. In such cases, project evaluators should proceed with caution. Unbundling is a useful analytic discipline, but it may be counterproductive to do it too explicitly. In our experience, managers often indulge in this kind of bundling to gain approval for genuinely worthwhile projects that are hard to justify in their own right. If they are forced to quantify the benefits of each subproject separately, some good projects may never see the light of day.

What gets included in or excluded from a project also depends on the proposers' need to end up with financial forecasts that are good enough to gain acceptance but not so good as to become an embarrassment later. It is often assumed that managers use optimistic revenue and cost projections if the project

Some investments are really two. Do you analyze them separately?

doesn't look profitable enough and do the opposite if it looks too profitable. According to our research, managers are in fact more likely to influence the numbers by redefining the project's boundaries.[5] They realize this is less likely to give hostages to fortune.

A highly profitable project will tend to be justified on the basis of its direct benefits but may also carry many indirect costs for such things as new computers or site refurbishment. Conversely, the proposer of a marginal project will tie in as many direct, quantifiable benefits as he or she can and exclude all indirect costs. This way, managers get corporate support for most of their projects without seriously compromising the decision-making process.

The management team at Fashion Bathrooms recognized the importance of project unbundling. Project Lightweight offered cost savings through a reduction in raw materials costs. On the other hand, it also promised quality improvements that would lead to increased sales. The CEO asked the finance director to rework the figures to determine if the project could be justified on the basis of cost savings alone—a benefit much easier to measure than incremental sales growth.

Unfortunately, cost savings alone were not enough. The project made sense only if the quality improvements could boost sales. This realization provoked further soul-searching. The managers reevaluated the quality improvements and asked themselves what evidence they had that sales would in fact benefit.

The quality improvements were twofold. First, the new bathtubs would be thinner and 35% lighter, making them easier to transport and install. Since plumbers and builders often make the buying decision, this feature was important. Second, the new casting process would create a smoother, shinier finish. But would these improvements really lead to more sales?

Fashion Bathrooms responded to this classic marketing problem by conducting market research. The results were revealing. Some people found many advantages in cast-iron bathtubs: they didn't flex and pull away from the wall, they looked better than shiny plastic, and they were more durable. But some complained of having to choose between a white cast-iron bathtub and a 20-week wait for a colored one. Others didn't even know that cast-iron bathtubs were available and that they had some advantages over plastic.

Would customers value the planned quality improvements? A lighter tub might seem less solid; a shiny finish might make it look just like a plastic tub. The evidence was shaky.

Ultimately Better Investments

In the end, Fashion Bathrooms shelved Project Lightweight. When managers scrutinized the analysis itself–not just the numbers it produced–they considered a new set of questions: Does Fashion Bathrooms have a sustainable competitive advantage? Why do people buy a particular type of bathtub? Was the company delivering what the market wanted, when it wanted it? And was Fashion Bathrooms helping to create a strong brand image for quality cast-iron bathtubs? These are the issues that are most important to strategic marketing.

When Fashion Bathrooms answered the questions and redid the financial analysis, things fell into place. The numbers demonstrated the benefits of investing

> When finance and marketing conflict, retrace the analysis.

in intangible assets like brand image, market position, customer franchise, and distribution channels, and of investing to improve factory organization, styling, production control, color mix, and, above all, delivery.

The Fashion Bathrooms story illustrates that in marketing and operations, detail matters. Good investments come from a detailed understanding of both the market and the company's operating and competitive capabilities. Used sensibly, finance helps bring these into the open. Financial analysis also helps clarify the project's boundaries by addressing issues like the base case, the time horizon, and future strategic options–all of which are as much strategic and market based as they are financial. Finance gives them a common language and framework.

Unfortunately, the financial analysis is all too often "pinned on" afterward, rather like the tail on the donkey in the children's game. An interactive process that relates the product-market specifics to the wider financial implications is not only a requirement for sound strategic investment decisions but also a powerful source of organizational learning.

Reprint 89502

Pitfalls in evaluating risky projects

Good analysis depends not only on techniques, but also on key assumptions

James E. Hodder and Henry E. Riggs

Recent critics of American business are wont to claim that our managers rely too heavily on a few financial techniques in weighing major investment decisions. Calculation of discounted cash flows, internal rates of return, and net present values, say the critics, is inherently biased against long-term investments. According to the authors of this article, the technicians, not the techniques, are the problem. Discounting procedures are not inherently biased if management sets realistic hurdle rates and examines carefully its own assumptions. Unfortunately, many DCF analyses of risky projects are overly simplistic and ignore three critical issues that managers and decision makers should consider: the effects of inflation, the different levels of uncertainty in different phases of a project, and management's own ability to mitigate risk.

Mr. Hodder is assistant professor of industrial engineering and engineering management at Stanford University. His teaching and research have focused on capital budgeting and international hedging decisions.

Mr. Riggs is professor of industrial engineering and engineering management and vice president for development at Stanford University. Before joining the university in 1974, he worked for 15 years in industry in various financial positions. Riggs is the author of many publications on accounting and finance and of the recent book, Managing High-Technology Companies *(Belmont, California, Lifetime Learnings Publications, a division of Wadsworth, Inc., 1983).*

In recent years, the leaders of American companies have been barraged with attacks on their investment policies. Critics accuse American executives of shortsightedness and point out that managers in Japan and Europe often fix their vision on more distant horizons. Here, it is claimed, managers pay too much attention to quarterly earnings reports and not enough to such basic elements of industrial strength as research and development. Some analysts see the root of this problem in the tendency of American companies to rely on discounted cash flow techniques in weighing long-term investments.[1] These critics argue that DCF techniques have inherent weaknesses that make them inappropriate for evaluating projects whose payoffs will come years down the road.

We disagree with the contention that DCF techniques are inappropriate for evaluating long-term or strategic investment proposals. We do believe, however, that companies often misapply or misinterpret DCF techniques. Misuse is particularly serious in evaluating long-term capital investments, such as ambitious R&D projects, that appear to involve high risk.

Misapplication of DCF techniques can certainly contribute to an unwarranted aversion to making long-term investments. However, the problem lies not in the technique but in its misuse. Money has a time value in every economy, and cash is the lifeblood of every business. To evaluate cash flows (costs or revenues) generated in different periods requires a procedure for making comparisons. For evaluating and ranking investment proposals, whether they have short or long lives, and involve capital equipment, R&D, or marketing expenditures, we need techniques that recognize that cash flows occur at different times. Discounting provides a rational and conceptually sound procedure for making such evaluations.

1 See, for example, Robert H. Hayes and David A. Garvin, "Managing as if Tomorrow Mattered," HBR May-June 1982, p. 71.

Unfortunately DCF techniques, like computers, can yield impressive-looking but misleading outputs when the inputs are flawed. Managers with biased assumptions may end up with biased conclusions. The fault, however, lies not with the technique but with the analyst. The path to improved capital budgeting requires education in the proper use of rational techniques rather than their rejection out of hand.

In our view, DCF techniques provide valuable information to *assist* management in making sound investment decisions. We emphasize the word assist because it is people, rather than analytical tools, who make decisions. Managers may have many objectives and face many constraints in their decision making. Nevertheless, they need information on the relative financial merits of different options. Properly employed, DCF techniques provide such information. The alternative is to ignore the time value of money and implicitly assume that, for example, a dollar earned ten years from now will have the same value as a dollar today.

DCF procedures, as commonly applied, are subject to three serious pitfalls:

Improper treatment of inflation effects, particularly in long-lived projects.

Excessive risk adjustments, particularly when risk declines in later phases of a project.

Failure to acknowledge how management can reduce project risk by diversification and other responses to future events.

Awareness of these pitfalls should help managers avoid uncritical use of DCF techniques that may lead to poor decisions.

An R&D project, for example

Although the comments here apply to a variety of investment proposals, we shall illustrate these three major pitfalls with the analysis of an R&D project. (*Exhibit I* lists examples of other investment projects that are frequently misevaluated for the reasons described in this article.) Because of their risk characteristics, R&D projects present some especially thorny problems. The pronounced uncertainties in these projects affect the analysis of risk in many ways.

Exhibit I	**Long-term risky investments frequently misevaluated**
1	A consumer goods company considers test marketing the first of a proposed new family of products.
2	A paper company studies investment in a new processing technique that could revolutionize paper making.
3	A drug company looks at increasing its investment in bio-medical research and the pilot plant that will be required if the research is successful.
4	A real estate developer analyzes the first-stage investment in improvements at a greenfield site for industrial-commercial facilities.
5	A financial services firm considers investment in a tele-communications facility that could radically alter the future distribution of its services.
6	A natural resources company evaluates a mineral-rights lease of a site that will require extensive development.

As a result, R&D projects with acceptable – even exciting – risk/return profiles may fail to meet the payoff criteria that management has established.

Let's look at a typical (hypothetical) project that would be rejected on the basis of the incomplete DCF analysis common in industry today. Then we'll show how a more complete and careful analysis reveals the project to be not only acceptable but highly desirable.

Our project has three distinct phases, as shown in *Exhibit II.* If the research (Phase 1) is successful, the project moves to market development (Phase 2), after which the resulting product may enjoy a long and profitable period of production and sales. The research and market development phases are periods of investment; returns are forthcoming only during the third period (Phase 3) when the product is sold.

It is important to differentiate between these phases, since each has decidedly different risk characteristics. Market development (Phase 2) will not be undertaken unless the research (Phase 1) is successful; thus, considerable uncertainty disappears before Phase 2 proceeds. Similarly, the sales period (Phase 3) follows only after successful results from research and market development. The information from Phase 2 will refine market projections, and Phase 3 cash flows are relatively low risk. In sum, uncertainty about the project diminishes progressively as we acquire more information.

According to the probabilities shown in *Exhibit II,* the project viewed as a whole (rather than by phases) has the expected-value cash flows shown in *Exhibit III* and an expected internal rate of return (IRR) slightly over 10%. This appears distinctly unattractive, even ridiculous, when compared with customary rates of return (hurdle rates) of 20% or more for high-risk projects. Given this analysis and results, most managers would almost certainly reject the project unless other strategic reasons dictated the investment.

Exhibit II	**Project description**		

Phase 1	**Research or product development**		
	$ 18 million annual research cost for 2 years		
	60 % probability of success		
Phase 2	**Market development**		
	Undertaken only if product development succeeds		
	$ 10 million annual expenditure for 2 years on the development of marketing and the establishment of marketing and distribution channels (net of any revenues earned in test marketing)		
Phase 3	**Sales**		
	Proceeds only if Phase 1 and Phase 2 verify opportunity		
	Production is subcontracted		
	The results of Phase 2 (available at the end of year 4) identify the product's market potential as shown below:		

Product demand	Product life	Annual net cash inflow	Probability
High	20 years	$ 24 million	.3
Medium	10 years	$ 12 million	.5
Low	Abandon project	None	.2

Note:
For simplicity, we assume that production is subcontracted in Phase 3 and that all cash flows are after tax and occur at year end. This assumption permits us to ignore some potentially complex tax issues involving depreciation and financing strategies. While a radical departure from reality, this assumption allows us to focus on issues of cash flow timing and risk that appear to be less widely understood.

Exhibit III	**Expected cash flows for the project** in $ millions	

Years	Expected value calculations	
1		− 18
2		− 18
3	.6 (− 10)	= − 6
4	.6 (− 10)	= − 6
5-14	.6 (.3 x 24 + .5 x 12)	=7.92
15-24	.6 (.3 x 24)	=4.32
Expected IRR = 10.1 %		

Many (if not most) U.S. companies, unfortunately, would probably analyze the project in this way, concluding that it is indeed risky and has an expected IRR below normal hurdle rates. The interpretation of these "facts" is far from obvious, however, and requires a deeper understanding of DCF calculation procedures. The issue is not which buttons to push on a calculator, but rather the appropriate interpretation of the inputs and consequent output since the DCF procedure is no more than a processing technique. The analysis appears sophisticated with its use

of probabilities and discounting, but it is incomplete and seriously misleading.

Adjusting for inflation

The most obvious shortcoming of the analysis is that it ignores how inflation will affect the various cash flows. At one extreme, they may not be affected at all. On the other hand, the cash flows may adjust directly and completely with inflation, that is, an 8% inflation rate next year will raise cash flows in that and following years by 8%. Most likely, inflation will affect different components of the cash flows in different ways and, when aggregated, the cash flows will adjust partially with inflation. Meaningful interpretation of the calculated IRR requires knowledge of this inflation adjustment pattern.

If complete adjustment were anticipated, the calculated IRR would represent an expected real return. However, comparing such real returns with nominal hurdle rates – including inflation – or nominal investment yields (for example, from government bonds) is not appropriate.[2] Historically, real yields on low-risk investments have averaged less than 5%, and the real yield on short-term U.S. Treasury securities has equalled close to zero. For higher risk investments, a frequent standard of comparison is the return (including dividends) on the Standard & Poor's "500" stock index. Over a 53-year period (1926-1978) the real rate of return on the S&P "500" averaged 8.5%. While we cannot be certain that history will repeat itself, long-run averages do provide one standard for comparison. Since listed securities represent an alternative investment, projects of comparable risk reasonably should have expected returns at least as great.

Returning to our hypothetical project, if cash flows adjust fully with inflation, the project offers a real return greater than the historic 8.5% of the S&P "500."

Many types of cash flows, of course, do not adjust fully with inflation, and some do not adjust at all. For example, depreciation tax shields, many lease payments, fixed-rate borrowing (like debentures), and multiyear fixed-price purchase or sales contracts do not change with the inflation rate. Consequently, a proper analysis requires an understanding of the inflation adjustment patterns for different cash flow segments.

2 James C. Van Horne, "A Note on Biases in Capital Budgeting Introduced by Inflation,"   *Journal of Financial and Quantitative Analysis,* January 1971, p. 653.

While American managers' awareness of the impact of inflation on project evaluation has risen in the last decade, even today many of them have at best a cursory understanding of it. Failure to incorporate inflation assumptions in DCF analyses can be particularly troublesome in decentralized companies. Corporate financial officers commonly specify companywide or divisional hurdle rates based on a current (nominal) cost of capital. Furthermore, analysts at the plant or division level often estimate future cash flows (particularly cost savings) based on current experience. Unless those analysts consciously include anticipated inflation, they will underestimate future cash flows and, unfortunately, many good projects may be rejected.

Parenthetically, the converse is unlikely to occur: it is hard to conceive of an analyst using inflated cash flows with real discount or hurdle rates. Also, projects that go forward usually undergo several reviews that are likely to result in some tempering, or lowering, of overly optimistic cash flow assumptions. By contrast, rejected projects are seldom given subsequent reviews that might reveal unrealistically low inflation assumptions.

The mismatch of inflation assumptions regarding cash flows and hurdle rates is generally most pronounced for projects with payoffs years down the road. So long as the inflation rate is positive (even if declining), the gap between projected real cash flows and their nominal equivalents grows with time. For example, suppose that inflation rates for the next three years are expected to be 8, 6, and 4% respectively. Consider an item that sells for $1 now. If its price will increase at the rate of inflation, its nominal price should be $1.08 next year, $1(1.08)(1.06) = $1.14 in two years, and $1(1.08)(1.06)(1.04) = $1.19 in three years. These inflated prices, rather than the current $1 price, should be incorporated into the DCF analysis if discounting is to occur at nominal rather than real interest rates.

The error that arises from the failure to include inflation in cash flow estimates compounds with time as long as inflation is positive. Under these circumstances, distant cash flows, such as those characteristic of research and development investments, have present values that are more seriously understated. It is difficult to know how widespread such errors have been during recent years, but almost surely they explain in part the shift toward shorter lived projects and myopic investment decisions in many businesses.

Avoiding excessive risk adjustments

A second flaw in the original DCF calculations for our hypothetical R&D project is the use of a single discount rate (IRR) for a project in which risk declines dramatically over time. As a result, the project appears less attractive than it really is. If we make appropriate adjustments for the differing risks in different stages of the project, the investment becomes much more attractive.

A typical discount rate (k) used in DCF analyses may be viewed as composed of three parts: a risk-free time value of money (RF), a premium for expected inflation (Eπ), and a risk premium (Δ) that increases with project risk. This relationship can be represented as:

$$1 + k = (1 + RF)(1 + E\pi)(1 + \Delta)$$

For example, a risk-free rate of 3% with 10% expected inflation and a 6% risk premium would imply $1 + k = (1.03)(1.10)(1.06) = 1.20$, or a nominal discount rate of approximately 20%.

Since inflation, as well as project risk and even the risk-free rate (RF), can vary over time, we should permit k to have different values at different times. The subscript t indicates the relevant time period; thus k_t is a function of the RF_t, $E\pi_t$, and Δ_t values for that period. To focus on situations where project risk is expected to change significantly through time, we will use real (deflated) cash flows and real discount rates with RF constant. It is, of course, very important to adjust for expected inflation properly. Without losing sight of that point, let's shift the focus of discussion to risk adjustments by assuming that the inflation adjustments have been executed properly.

Denoting the real (risky) discount rate for period t as r_t, we have:

$$1 + r_t = (1 + RF)(1 + \Delta_t)$$

This differs from k_t simply by the removal of the inflation factor $(1 + E\pi_t)$. Then by definition, the NPV of a project with expected real cash flows (CF_t) occurring in two periods is:

$$NPV = \frac{CF_1}{1 + r_1} + \frac{CF_2}{(1 + r_1)(1 + r_2)}$$

$$= \frac{CF_1}{(1 + RF)(1 + \Delta_1)}$$

$$+ \frac{CF_2}{(1 + RF)^2(1 + \Delta_1)(1 + \Delta_2)}$$

This brings us to a key point. If $\Delta_1 = \Delta_2 = \Delta$, this formula collapses into the familiar form with a single discount rate:

$$NPV = \frac{CF_1}{(1 + RF)(1 + \Delta)} + \frac{CF_2}{(1 + RF)^2(1 + \Delta)^2}$$

$$= \frac{CF_1}{1 + r} + \frac{CF_2}{(1 + r)^2}$$

In practice, virtually all DCF calculations are performed using a constant discount rate such as r. Indeed, financial calculators are programmed that way. Under what conditions, however, can we assume that $\Delta_1 = \Delta_2$ (even approximately)?

This assumption is reasonable if we anticipate that errors in predicting real cash flows result from a random walk process–that is, predictions one period into the future always entail the same uncertainty. Thus if we were at time 1, each dollar of real cash flow in period 2 would look just as risky as each dollar of CF_1 looks now. However, predicting two periods into the future is more risky; thus CF_2 viewed from the present deserves a larger risk adjustment. Consequently, CF_2 is multiplied by $1/(1 + \Delta)^2$ as opposed to simply $1/(1 + \Delta)$ for CF_1. In more general terms, the risk adjustment factor for a cash flow t period in the future is $1/(1 + \Delta)^t$. The risk adjustment grows geometrically with time.

Using a single risk-adjusted discount rate, therefore, implies an important and somewhat special assumption about the risks associated with future cash flow estimates: such risks increase geometrically with chronological distance from the present. On the infrequent occasions when this assumption is mentioned, it is usually justified on the grounds that the accuracy of our foresight decreases with time. While that argument has merit, consider what can happen when an investment proposal does not fit this pattern.

Recall our R&D project. If the cash flows of *Exhibit II* are in real terms, the project has an expected real IRR of 10%; but there is a 40% chance of investing $36 million (real, after tax, but undiscounted) during the first two years and receiving nothing. Many decision makers would demand a much higher return than 10% (real or otherwise) to undertake such an investment. If the project proceeds to Phase 3, the cash flows in that phase are considered relatively low risk. The large risk adjustments that were appropriate for early phases are no longer appropriate once we reach Phase 3.

To highlight this point, let's suppose that Phase 3 could be sold if the project successfully proceeds through the first two phases. Given its low risk, potential investors might evaluate Phase 3 with a low discount rate such as 5% (real). Suppose market research reveals a high demand for the product during

Phase 3: 20-year life with annual net cash inflows of $24 million. Discounting these flows at 5%, we reach a value at the beginning of Phase 3 (end of year 4) of $299 million. Thus if strong demand develops for the product, it's possible the rights to produce and market it could be sold for a considerable sum. This value depends, however, on the marketing results from Phase 2. Thus we need to check what happens if less favorable demand conditions are revealed in Phase 2. Performing similar calculations for the other possible market conditions, we obtain the values in *Exhibit IV.*

Even though there is a 20% chance of low demand, the overall expected value of selling Phase 3 is $136 million. Suppose we now recalculate the project's expected IRR assuming such an outright sale of Phase 3 for its expected value: $136 million. Using the 60% probability of Phase 1 success, we calculate the expected cash flows to be those in *Exhibit V.* Those net expected cash flows are equivalent to an expected IRR of approximately 28%. In other words, the prospect that Phase 3 could be sold as just discussed leads us to revise the overall expected IRR for investing in the project from 10 up to 28%. Since these calculations are in real terms, the project now appears quite attractive.

Pushing this analysis one step further, let's assume the project could also be sold at the end of Phase 1 if the research is successful. That is, the new owner after purchasing the project would pay an estimated $10 million per year of Phase 2 costs and receive the Phase 3 value (depending on marketing research results) as shown in *Exhibit IV.* The purchaser would now encounter the expected cash flows indicated in *Exhibit VI.*

Clearly this proposition is riskier than just buying Phase 3, since the marketing research results of Phase 2 are not yet known. Suppose a potential purchaser evaluated the cash flows in *Exhibit VI* using a 20% discount rate (well over twice the historic real return on the S&P "500"). The implied purchase price (present value at the beginning of Phase 2) is slightly over $79 million. But what is the implied return to the first owner–the initial developer of the product who undertakes the risky proposition of investing $18 million for each of two years in research–if a successful project could be sold at the end of two years for $79 million? The expected real return (including the 40% chance of Phase 1 failure) is over 63% –a far cry from our initial estimate.

This analysis illustrates a pitfall in evaluating projects with risk patterns that differ significantly from the simple random walk assumption. In our example, uncertainty is greatest during the first two years. But it is unreasonable to penalize more than 20 years of subsequent cash flows for that risk. To dramatize this point, we have assumed that the project can be sold in its latter phases. Indeed, the project acquires a dramatically high value if Phase 1 succeeds—a point missed by the initial IRR calculation, which implicitly discounted all cash flows at the same rate.

The difficulty with using a single risk-adjusted discount rate (or IRR) is that the analysis blends time discount and risk adjustment factors. Unless project risk follows a simple random walk pattern, this blending is inappropriate. Although this problem is discussed in the academic literature,[3] it is generally ignored in practice. For projects with dramatically different risk phases, the result can be a serious misestimation of project value.

A more appropriate procedure for evaluating such projects is to separate timing and risk adjustments using the concept of certainty equivalent value (CEV). The CEV of a cash flow in a given year is simply its risk-adjusted value in that year. If we converted all future cash flows to CEVs, we could then discount the CEVs to the present using a single risk-free discount rate. With the timing and risk adjustments thus separated, we avoid the possibility of compounding risk adjustments unintentionally.

As a practical matter, attempting to convert each year's cash flow into a CEV can be cumbersome since the CEV for period t may depend on probabilities for cash flows in the previous period (t-1), which in turn depend on probabilities from t-2, and so on. In our example, the cash flows in Phase 3 depend on results from Phases 1 and 2. Indeed, we have assumed that management would abandon the project altogether if the research is unsuccessful or market tests indicate low demand.

Although it is important to consider interactions among cash flows in different periods, the analysis of all possible management responses or other contingencies would be extraordinarily complex and unwieldy. Thus we need reasonable approximations. Managers and analysts must exercise judgment regarding which risks and possible actions should be included in the analysis. We recommend that high-risk projects be evaluated as a sequence of distinct risk phases (of perhaps several years each).

In our example, we did not attempt to calculate CEVs for each year in Phase 3. Rather, we estimated a value for the whole phase conditional on the demand level. Similarly, our calculated $79 million value for the project if Phase 1 succeeded is a CEV (at the beginning of year three) for Phases 2 and 3 combined. In both cases, these CEVs are estimates of the project's potential selling price—its market value at the end of years two and four respectively. While the project might be worth more to the company if it retained all phases, the market CEVs represent opportunity

Exhibit IV	**Anticipated Phase 3 values if sold** in $ millions		
Demand	Probability	Value of Phase 3 year 4	
High	.3	299	
Medium	.5	93	
Low	.2	0	
Expected value =		136	

Exhibit V	**Expected cash flows with Phase 3 sale** in $ millions		
Year	Outflow	Inflow	Net
1	−18		−18
2	−18		−18
3	−10 x .6		−6
4	−10 x .6	136 x .6	75.6

Exhibit VI	**Expected cash flows for purchaser of Phase 2** in $ millions		
Year	Outflow	Inflow	Net
3	−10		−10
4	−10	136	126

Exhibit VII	**Expected cash flows if the project can be abandoned during Phase 1** in $ millions		
Year	Expected outflow	Expected inflow	Expected net cash flow
1	−18		−18
2	−18 x .8	79 x .6	33

costs for retaining Phases 2 and 3 that are useful (and conservative) yardsticks for evaluating the entire project.

Estimating market values for different phases is obviously an imprecise process. Using a single risk-adjusted rate for an entire phase (rather than separate rates or CEVs for each cash flow) produces only an approximation, unless risks within that phase have a random walk pattern. The approximation is reasonable, however, if the discount rate is low and/or the phase covers a fairly short period of time (as in Phases 1 and 2 above). If a phase is both long and risky, analysts should divide it into subphases.

To restate our argument, we recommend segmenting projects into risk phases, then valu-

3 See, for example, Alexander A. Robichek and Stewart C. Myers, "Conceptual Problems in the Use of Risk-Adjusted Discount Rates," *Journal of Finance,* December 1966, p. 727.

ing sequentially each phase, working backward from the last. This procedure can be used to determine either an expected IRR on the initial phase (as already illustrated) or an NPV for the project. In general, we prefer calculating NPVs since this avoids technical problems with IRR, including scale ambiguities. Although slightly more complex than a standard expected NPV or IRR calculation, our approach is not difficult per se. It simply entails a short sequence of expected NPV calculations using different interest rates to value different risk phases. When a project's risk pattern differs substantially from the simple random walk assumption, such differences should be recognized and the evaluation procedure modified accordingly. As we have shown, evaluation based on inappropriate analysis can be very misleading.

Considering the eye of the beholder

A third major problem in project evaluations is correctly assessing project risk and how managers can influence its nature and level. Here it is important to consider the perspective of the analyst. Risk that seems excessive to an R&D or project manager may appear reasonable to a corporate executive or a shareholder who can diversify the risk by spreading it across other investments. Also, managers can influence the level of risk by future actions that affect the ultimate payoff of a project investment.

Frequently, the major uncertainty in R&D investments is whether the research phase will produce a viable product. From the perspective of financial market theories such as the Capital Asset Pricing Model (CAPM), risks associated with the research phase are apt to be largely diversifiable. Consequently, a public shareholder with a well-diversified securities portfolio will probably voice little or no concern about these risks. Success or failure in the lab is probably correlated weakly (if at all) with broad economic forces or other systematic nondiversifiable factors that affect returns in the stock market as a whole.

The CAPM and related theories stress that a project's total risk normally contains both diversifiable and nondiversifiable components. To the extent shareholders can easily diversify their holdings in the financial markets, they can reduce *their* portion of the project's diversifiable risk to a very small level. Under these circumstances, the shareholders need worry only about the systematic portion of project risk. Thus a financial market approach suggests that the typical R&D project is much less risky from the perspective of a well-diversified public shareholder

Calculating inflation's effects

To correctly allow for inflation in a DCF analysis, some analysts include it in the cash flows and use nominal discount rates. If inflation rates are expected to vary, different discount rates can be used for different years in a net present value (NPV) calculation. Such a procedure, however, entails cumbersome calculations. Furthermore, consistency on a companywide basis requires specifying the annual series of discount and inflation rates to be used by analysts. The simple approach is to use a single "average" inflation rate with a single nominal discount rate, but this is not ideal. Although in many cases the distortion associated with this approximation is not serious, the pattern of cash flows and projected inflation affects the size of the distortion.

A preferable procedure is to use deflated cash flows with real discount rates. In this approach, analysts estimate the cash flow in each period, including the increase from inflation applicable to each of its segments (for example, zero for depreciation tax shields). Analysts then deflate the cash flow to present (for example, 1985) dollars using the projected inflation between now and that period. If the cash flow is expected to adjust fully with inflation, the deflation adjustment will exactly cancel the included inflation. If not, the real value of that future cash flow will be altered by the extent to which it does not fully adjust with inflation. The series of deflated (real) cash flows can then be discounted using real discount rates. Since the real time value of money appears to be considerably more stable than its nominal counterpart, this second procedure is superior to using a single nominal discount rate.

than it may appear to the individual performing the DCF analysis.

In contrast, managers, creditors, and even suppliers may focus on total risk (including both diversifiable and systematic components) at the company level. These groups have interests that are not easily diversified in the sense that the CAPM assumes. Thus they are concerned about total cash flow variability but at the company (not project) level. Even at the company level, however, the R&D budget may be spread across many projects. A multi-industry company of even moderate size is probably sufficiently diversified to allow large reductions in cash flow variability per dollar of R&D investment. Once again, the risk of a particular project appears lower from a portfolio perspective than from the perspective of an analyst looking only at the project itself.

Most managers are aware of portfolio effects and the arguments regarding shareholder welfare based on financial market models such as the CAPM. Nevertheless, it is understandable that they view a project with over a 50% chance of no payoff (as in our example) as highly risky. Under such circumstances, it is easy to ignore portfolio effects and worry too much about the risk of that particular investment opportunity. This excessive risk aversion is frequently manifested in a too-high discount or hurdle rate, thus compounding the pitfalls already discussed.

Analysts may also use conservative estimates: overestimates of development time or costs and underestimates of both the magnitude and duration of subsequent payoffs. Although the tendency toward excessive conservatism is both inevitable and difficult to overcome, management needs to be aware of its existence and sensitive to its consequences. As we said earlier, projects that have been rejected are seldom reevaluated. It is all too easy for a good project to be lost.

While excessive risk adjustments are certainly not unique to R&D proposals, the problem may be more severe here because R&D projects involve large and obvious uncertainties. The key is that these risks are likely to be highly diversifiable. Failure to recognize this fact represents a systematic bias against R&D projects.

Managers can also affect the level of risk by influencing the distribution of project payoffs. In our example, there is a 30% chance that Phase 3 will be worth $299 million. There is not a symmetric chance of losing $299 million – because the company will abandon the project if faced with low product demand. The result is an *expected* value for Phase 3 ($136 million) which is $43 million above the *most likely* estimate of $93 million. Unfortunately, many project evaluations consider only the most likely cash flow estimates and ignore the asymmetry or skewness of the payoffs. This practice understates the project's true value in situations in which future management actions can improve profits or limit losses.

This problem is more significant for R&D projects than for other investments because the company has greater flexibility to expand production for highly successful products and to abandon apparently unprofitable efforts. Such managerial actions can result in greater returns than estimated originally (larger revenues over a longer period) as well as reduced downside risk.

In our example, suppose progress can be monitored throughout Phase 1, and management has the option to abandon the project at the end of the first year if certain goals are not met. If the probability of research failure is equally divided between years one and two (20% each), the expected IRR from an initial investment in Period 1 research increases from 63% to 83%, with no change in our other assumptions (*Exhibit VII* shows the relevant cash flows). Clearly management's ability to skew a payoff distribution in the company's favor can have an important influence on a project's desirability.

DCF analysis in perspective

How much the misuse of DCF techniques has contributed to the competitive troubles of American companies is a matter of conjecture. It is clear, though, that incomplete analysis can severely penalize investments whose payoffs are both uncertain and far in the future. Given these perils, one might argue that DCF procedures should be avoided or should be accorded little weight in long-term investment decisions. We strongly disagree. It is foolish to ignore or to indict useful analytical tools simply because they might be used incorrectly or incompletely. Rather, analysts and decision makers should recognize potential problems and be careful to ensure that evaluations are performed correctly. Managers cannot treat a DCF evaluation like a black box, looking only at the output. They need to break open the box, examine the assumptions inside, and determine how those assumptions affect the analysis of a project's long-term profitability.

DCF procedures can help evaluate the implications of altered price, cost, or timing assumptions, but managers must first specify the correct assumptions. These procedures can also be used to examine the effects of different capacity expansion or R&D strategies under many scenarios. However, again managers must specify the strategies or scenarios to be examined. In short, discounting is only one step in evaluating alternative investment opportunities. This fact has frequently been lost in the arguments (pro and con) about the use of discounting procedures.

Blaming DCF procedures for short-sightedness, biased perceptions, excessive risk aversion, or other alleged management weaknesses does not address the underlying problems of American industry. However, understanding the pitfalls in the casual use of DCF techniques can both improve the analysis of capital investment projects and place these techniques in a more appropriate perspective.

It is important to remember that managers make decisions. DCF techniques can assist in that process, but they are only tools. Correctly used, these techniques provide a logical and consistent framework for comparing cash flows occurring at different times – an important aspect of virtually every investment project. ▽

Assessing capital risk: you can't be too conservative

Jasper H. Arnold III

"Worst case forecasts are almost always too optimistic."

In the summer of 1981, the top officers of the Cloud Tool Company, a large oil-field equipment manufacturer, were nervous about borrowing $15 million from their bank to finance a large plant expansion. They had chosen this investment over several smaller ones because it would enable the company to hold onto, or even raise, its share of the rapidly growing, and continually profitable, energy market. To ensure that the company was not assuming too much risk, the financial staff did a worst case forecast. The forecast showed that – even under adverse circumstances – the company had enough cash to repay the debt.

By late 1982, management nervousness had turned to fear. The oil business had fallen into a severe recession, the company had reported large losses, and cash generation had dropped. A principal payment on the bank loan was due at the end of the year, and the finance VP had projected that the company would not have enough cash on hand. A default would mean that the bank could foreclose on the pledged assets or force an involuntary bankruptcy. Only then did the managers realize that their worst case scenario had been much too optimistic. If they had opted for a more modest expansion, the existence of their company probably would not be in jeopardy.

Many managers don't realize that when they finance a large expansion project with debt, they may be assuming far too much risk. High profit potential, personal commitment to the project, or faith in the industry can hamper executives' vision of the future. They want it to be rosy, so they avoid acknowledging that a crisis could occur. But if the project incurs large

Jasper Arnold is a senior vice president and manager of the credit department at First City National Bank of Houston. This is his second article for HBR. His first, "How to Negotiate a Term Loan," appeared in March-April 1982.

losses, the company's financial resources and flexibility can waste away. At the extreme, the company can fail. A critical part of capital budgeting should be a realistic – and conservative – worst case analysis.

When a company gets into trouble, lending banks do a staying power analysis. It is a conservative way to assess the company resources available to repay loans under distressed circumstances. To see how well their company could withstand financial setbacks, managers can also use this method before embarking on a capital expansion program. Then if they want to bet the company, at least they know that's what they're doing.

As a banker at a large New York bank and now at a regional bank in Texas, I have been involved in the financing of many capital expenditure programs. I have also turned down requests. In every case, I have heard management justify the investment and have seen the supporting analysis. Over time, I have seen the outcomes of their decisions. These experiences have taught me that:

Most large capital expenditure programs encounter large problems.

These problems can be financially destructive if the company has invested on too grand a scale.

Without a realistic worst case scenario, managers often don't appreciate the amount of risk their companies assume.

Staying power analysis helps managers both evaluate worst case performance and decide on a project's size.

When undertaking a large expansion program, management usually acknowledges that it might face some short-term reversals or minor problems, but it generally is convinced that nothing serious will happen and that the project will succeed. This optimism is unjustified. In fact, most projects – more than 50% by my estimate – encounter big setbacks. A Rand Corporation study found that the first construction-cost estimate of process plants involving new technology was usually less than half of the final cost, and many projects experience even worse performance. Research using PIMS data revealed that more than 80% of the new projects studied failed to achieve their market-share targets.[1]

My experience and discussions with other bankers and executives show that in at least one out of five projects, managers regret their investments because of large or persistent losses. An aircraft manufacturer, for example, undertook production of a new commercial jetliner. Its major subcontractor went bankrupt, and there was insufficient demand for the jetliner. The company suffered large losses and eventually had to terminate production. I have seen examples like this in the defense contracting, chemical, and microcomputer industries as well.

When worst cases look too good

Today's complex and treacherous business environment raises the chance that a company will encounter trouble. My experience in the last decade with companies in the energy industry motivated me, in large part, to write this article. What occurred there vividly illustrates the business environment's instability and the difficulties this creates in capital budgeting.

After the Arab oil embargo of 1973, the oil business enjoyed the strongest boom in its history. It lasted until the end of 1981 when the posted price of OPEC crude peaked at $34 per barrel. Companies made tremendous investments aimed at finding more oil and gas, and they financed many of these investments with debt. Some companies did implement smaller capital expenditure programs, but many leaned toward large, ambitious projects because of the tantalizing profits and the seemingly permanent nature of the boom.

In early 1982, the bubble burst. Because of the worldwide glut of oil and natural gas, OPEC had

to cut prices. The oil companies reduced their exploration activity, and a cataclysmic decline in profits ensued. A large number of companies went bankrupt, and many still teeter on the brink with cash flows barely above the level required to service debt.

The severely troubled energy companies share a common experience: management made capital expenditures that were far too large for the company's size, and it financed them with debt. When earnings are strong, companies may be able to service a large amount of debt, but when business activity and cash flow drop, principal and interest payments can be so large that the company cannot operate for long without defaulting on a loan. Under these circumstances, companies have little time to cut expenses or sell assets to generate cash, and lenders are usually unwilling to advance additional funds to companies they already view as too highly leveraged.

Cloud Tool Company's story is fairly typical. Its top management ignored a business tenet: the bigger the project, the more money it will lose if it gets in trouble. To make large capital expenditures, a business must be able to sustain large losses, either through earnings from other products or, if the company is undiversified, through a large equity base that can absorb the losses and still comfort the lenders by protecting their loans.

Unfortunately, the oil industry's experience is not unusual. The sky has fallen on many industries – textile manufacturing, chemical production, cement manufacturing, commercial real estate development, and home computer manufacturing – just when managers thought they had found the pot of gold at the end of the rainbow. Unstable energy cartels, rapid technological change, deregulation of protected industries, aggressive foreign competition, industry recessions, and legions of professional managers who are well schooled in exploiting their companies' strengths and attacking their competitors' weaknesses contribute to this uncertainty.

Most companies support large capital expenditure programs with a worst case analysis that examines the project's loss potential. But the worst case forecast is almost always too optimistic. When problems occur, the financial results are usually much worse than the predictions. When managers look at the downside, they generally describe a mildly pessimistic future rather than the worst possible future.

A worst case analysis conventionally entails preparing a pessimistic cash flow forecast to determine if operations can generate enough cash to repay debt according to its contractual terms. But this approach has some problems. First, a very pessimistic analysis often reveals that the company cannot service the debt at all, especially if the project is large for the company's size. This unhappy result tends to bias the forecaster toward only mild pessimism when divining

1 David Davis,
"New Projects:
Beware of False Economies,"
HBR March-April 1985, p. 95.

the future. Second, cash flow from operations is not necessarily the only source of cash for debt repayment during hard times; lenders will sometimes make additional loans or defer payments on existing debt. Finally, this approach does not indicate the costs of such lender assistance because it is not conducted from a lender's standpoint.

Staying power analysis is a better way to do a worst case forecast. When a borrower gets into financial trouble, bankers employ this technique to see how much additional money they can advance to cover cash deficits or if it would be prudent to defer principal payments until the company's health improves. Management can use staying power analysis to determine if the company can avoid a default on loans or other obligations and thereby avoid an involuntary bankruptcy, a lawsuit for payment, or a foreclosure on pledged assets. The technique can also help managers decide on the appropriate size of an important capital expenditure.

Lender's perspective

To conduct a staying power analysis, a manager must understand the lender's viewpoint. A cardinal rule of credit is to have two sources of repayment. The primary source of repayment is always the business's operating cash flow. If the most likely forecast shows that this source is inadequate, the lender will usually not make the loan. The secondary source of repayment is the liquidation value of assets; it comes into play when the company gets into trouble and can only generate a very low – or negative – cash flow.

If a company actually begins to show losses, however, and can't service debt from internal sources, lenders do not like to liquidate assets. Liquidation values are uncertain, and a forced bankruptcy or foreclosure is expensive and time-consuming and may tarnish the lender's competitive image. Lenders would rather work with management to keep the company alive so that repayment can ultimately come from cash generation. Such accommodations, however, are by no means automatic and may be costly. Lenders must have confidence in management's ability and must believe that the company has a good chance of returning to profitability. They must believe that the liquidation value of the assets representing their collateral is, or soon will be, equal to or greater than their outstanding loans. If asset coverage is inadequate, lenders are prone to move immediately against the assets before more losses further reduce their value.

The borrowing base is the maximum loan value that lenders ascribe to the company's assets. It is critical to staying power analysis. Here are some fairly representative borrowing-base values of assets normally considered acceptable collateral: accounts receivable are worth 80% of carrying value; inventory is worth 50% of carrying value; and land, buildings, and equipment are worth 90% of "orderly liquidation value" (the amount that could be realized in a piecemeal sale of the assets after a diligent search for interested buyers and an effort at negotiating a favorable price).

Accounts receivable must be fairly current and owed by financially sound companies. The type of inventory affects the amount of credit it will support. Commodity raw materials, such as petrochemical resins or steel scrap, have a readily determined market value and can be assigned a fairly high advance rate – usually 60% to 75% of cost. Finished goods such as consumer durables, where style is not a factor, or standard steel shapes may be similarly treated. Specialty raw materials or finished goods with a narrow market will have only a 25% to 50% advance rate. Work-in-process inventory rarely has any borrowing value.

Lenders frequently use outside appraisers to value fixed assets. In times of distress, lenders will usually advance 80% to 90% of orderly liquidation value. For analysis purposes, these values should be very low for special-purpose equipment or for large, special-purpose manufacturing plants that would have a limited resale value if an industry got into serious trouble or if a new manufacturing technology failed. Twenty-five to thirty cents on the cost dollar is not unreasonable. Your banker will confirm that such assets have sold for less.

"While you were out! Let's see. Oh, yes. Everybody in the office plunged into a state of despondency and funk, pending your return."

Analyze staying power

To illustrate how staying power analysis works, I will use the example of Acme Fabrication Company, an industrial product manufacturer. It reported 1985 sales of $35.1 million and net profits of $1.9 million. In early 1986, management was considering making a large addition to its plant that it hoped would dramatically raise sales. If it made the addition immediately, the cost of the fixed assets would be $12 million. The company could arrange financing in the form of a five-year bank term loan to be repaid in equal annual installments of principal.

Management also had the option of making the investment in phases: $6.5 million in 1986 and then, if things went as expected, another $6.8 million in 1987. Note that for the same amount of capacity the phased expansion was more expensive than the immediate, large investment: $13.3 million versus $12 million. This was because of inflation over two years and the cost economies in constructing and equipping the large-scale project. Another unattractive feature of the phased approach was the prospect of lower sales and earnings over the life of the project relative to the results of the large-scale option because by spending the money in increments the company could not achieve certain production and marketing economies.

The same bank would provide all existing and new debt, and the loans would initially be unsecured. The company had a $6.5 million line of credit at this bank and $3.9 million was outstanding in the form of notes payable.

Both options were analyzed from a strategic standpoint and were found acceptable. The company also used discounted cash flow hurdles, and both alternatives met the minimum standard.

Describe a hostile environment. Begin the staying power analysis by forecasting the financial performance that would result from the most hostile environment that might *reasonably* occur. I emphasize the word "reasonably" because one can paint such a bleak picture that survival is impossible. While not a pleasant task, describing a disaster scenario is fairly simple. For Acme, the chief risks were a steep industry recession and rising steel costs. Since the industry's cyclical swings did not always coincide with the ups and downs of steel prices, management thought that the company might have to contend with rising steel costs during an industrywide recession.

The forecaster then translates the description of the hostile operating environment into financial results. Nearly every risk predictably shows up in a company's financial statements. The impact of the

Exhibit I	Impact of hostile environment on Acme's financial statements	
	Risks	**Impact on financial statements**
	Steep industry recession	Declining prices due to falling unit sales volume and lower selling prices
		Slow inventory turnover due to excess or hard-to-move stock
		Slow accounts receivable collection period due to the effects of the recession on customers
	Rising raw materials costs	Rise in cost of goods sold because of higher steel costs and higher per unit manufacturing costs due to lower production volume

hostile environment on Acme's statements appears in *Exhibit I*.

Estimate erosion potential. Quantifying the duration of the bad period and the dollar magnitudes is the hardest part. With experience or good strategic risk analysis, management can usually estimate the range of outcomes for each affected financial statement account. When making these estimates, focus on each account's erosion potential: the most deterioration that might occur in the hostile operating environment. For some financial statement variables, thinking in absolute terms is convenient: "Accounts receivable collection period could conceivably rise to 120 days in a severe recession." For others, using percentages is handier: "Sales could fall by 30% over two years."

Historical results are a good source of information for estimating erosion potential, but a tranquil past often gives false comfort. In dynamic and evolving markets, the future may present obstacles never encountered before. Managers, therefore, should err on the conservative side and estimate results much worse than those seen in the past. If the worst historical sales performance has been a 25% drop over two years, management might run the forecast based on a 35% drop. In studying historical data, managers should go 10 or 15 years back if possible. They can also gain insights from studying the results of other companies in the industry.

The executives may have trouble admitting that some worst case scenarios are possible, but history shows that they do often happen. Therefore, if the purpose of the expansion is to turn out a new product, assume that unit sales volume is 60% to 85% of the levels your most likely projections assume. The exact discount will depend on the amount of market research and testing done, the competition's ability to retaliate or otherwise preclude you from achieving the anticipated market share, and other factors that might affect the risk of buyer acceptance.

If the purpose of the expansion is to employ new production technology, do what bankers do: run your projections assuming that the project never works and that the company must repay its debt from the base business's cash flows. If you ran a successful pilot plant or implemented other risk-reducing measures, assume large cost overruns and a long delay in reaching commercial production levels.

Don't ignore working capital. Managers without a financial orientation often ignore or drastically underestimate the total amount of money a project ultimately requires. They think in terms of fixed assets—land, building, and equipment—and do not think enough about the additional investment in net working capital. In Acme's case, the large-scale option required a $12 million fixed-asset investment but, as we will see shortly, the amount needed the first year to get the project under way was much more—$19.3 million. The company needed the additional $7.3 million because the new plant caused sales to rise, which led to higher accounts receivable and meant that more inventory had to be carried. A "spontaneous" rise in accounts payable and accrued liabilities automatically supplied part of the financing to support this, but an external source had to fund the balance. For most companies this source is debt, which increases leverage and, therefore, risk.

Include cost-cutting efforts. The forecaster must also anticipate what cash conservation programs the company would implement when financially distressed. Management would probably make these decisions:

Cut selling, general, and administrative (SG & A) expenses.

Sell marketable securities.

Reduce inventory levels.

Cut the dividend.

Reduce capital expenditures.

Sell unnecessary assets.

Delay paying vendors.

The company can only go so far with some of these actions. In preparing financial forecasts, managers often assume that sales drive many balance sheet and income statement accounts. For example, if sales drop by 10%, they assume a 10% decline in accounts receivable, inventory, selling, and general and administrative expenses. But when companies get into trouble this is usually not the case, especially at the onset of financial difficulty. Unsure how severe the situation will get or how long it will last, executives hesitate to reduce inventories or to cut SG&A expenses. And the company's financial condition has to deteriorate dramatically before management will consider firing people.

The same is true about cutting the dividend. Management wants to protect sensitive stockholders and show the stock market that all is well. Capital expenditures may not be easy to reduce either. Equipment-purchase or construction contracts may have been signed months before the problems arose, or the manufacturing process may ruin the equipment so that it must be frequently replaced. So it's best to assume that any big cuts will be delayed and slow to take effect. Moreover, SG&A expenses and capital spending cannot be cut beyond a certain point, and the sales force may be unable to get rid of excessive inventories if the bottom falls out of the market.

One more reality of hard times needs mentioning. I have seen many forecasts in which managers try to reflect a worst case scenario and assume a drop in sales but hold gross margins about in line with historical levels. In most industry recessions, what actually happens is this: declining sales volume stimulates price cutting, and as excess production capacity rises, price cutting becomes rampant as companies try to generate orders that at least cover out-of-pocket costs; as production is reduced to reflect the drop in sales, unit costs rise as fixed costs are spread over fewer units. The impact of this on gross profits is magnified because the falling sales prices and the rising unit costs squeeze the margin on each unit sold, and the company sells fewer units. To make matters worse, the company's customers usually take longer to pay because either they have the power of a buyer's market or they are also hurt by the recession and try to conserve cash.

Acme created its forecasts from these types of assumptions. Based on current backlog and market strength, management thought it reasonable to expect a good year in 1986 followed by a steep, two-year recession with drastically falling sales, shrinking profit margins, and a slowdown in inventory and receivables turnover. The company made the assumption that payables would be stretched and marketable securities sold to generate cash, but that it would delay big cuts in SG&A expenses and capital expenditures until 1988.

Exhibit II shows the staying power analysis for the large-scale project. The top part is the forecast income statement. A $1.5 million loss occurs in 1987 followed by a severe loss of $4.4 million in 1988; thereafter the company returns to profitability.

Exhibit II   **Acme's staying power analysis for a large project**
in millions of dollars*

			Actual	Projected				
			1985	1986	1987	1988	1989	1990
Income statement	Income and expenses	Net sales	$ 35.1	$ 61.1	$ 53.0	$ 43.0	$ 53.0	$ 56.0
		Cost of goods sold	24.6	44.5	43.4	39.4	40.9	42.4
		Gross profit	10.5	16.6	9.6	3.6	12.1	13.6
		Selling, general, and administrative expense	5.5	9.6	9.6	9.1	7.6	7.6
		Interest expense	1.5	2.9	2.8	2.6	2.4	2.0
		Profit before tax	3.5	4.1	− 2.8	− 8.1	2.1	4.0
		Income taxes	1.6	1.9	− 1.3	− 3.7	1.0	1.8
		Net income	**1.9**	**2.3**	**− 1.5**	**− 4.4**	**1.1**	**2.2**
Balance sheet	Assets	Cash and marketable securities	$ .4	$ .4	$ .3	$ .3	$ .3	$ .3
		Accounts receivable	5.8	10.0	9.1	7.7	9.0	9.2
		Inventory	8.8	15.3	15.0	14.5	14.0	14.5
		Current assets	**15.0**	**25.7**	**24.4**	**22.5**	**23.3**	**24.0**
		Net fixed assets	17.5	26.1	23.7	20.8	17.9	15.0
		Total assets	**32.5**	**51.8**	**48.1**	**43.3**	**41.2**	**39.0**
	Liabilities and stockholders' equity	Accounts payable and accrued liabilities	4.7	8.2	8.4	8.2	8.5	8.9
		Current maturities of long-term debt	1.0	3.4	3.4	3.4	3.4	3.4
		Notes payable (existing)	3.9	3.9	3.9	3.9	3.9	3.9
		Additional short-term debt	−	2.5	3.6	6.7	6.6	5.3
		Current liabilities	**9.6**	**18.0**	**19.3**	**22.2**	**22.4**	**21.5**
		Long-term debt	9.0	17.6	14.2	10.8	7.4	4.0
		Stockholders' equity	13.9	16.2	14.6	10.2	11.4	13.6
		Total liabilities and stockholders' equity	**32.5**	**51.8**	**48.1**	**43.3**	**41.2**	**39.0**
Sources and uses of cash	Sources	Net income		$ 2.3	$ −1.5	$ −4.4	$ 1.1	$ 2.2
		Depreciation		3.4	3.4	3.4	3.4	3.4
		Total sources		**5.7**	**1.9**	**− 1.0**	**4.5**	**5.6**
	Uses	Capital expenditures		12.0	1.0	.5	.5	.5
		Long-term debt repayment		1.0	3.4	3.4	3.4	3.4
		Change in net working capital†		7.3	− 1.5	− 1.7	.5	.4
		Total uses		**20.3**	**2.9**	**2.2**	**4.4**	**4.3**
		Cash flow before external financing (S-U)		−14.6	− 1.0	− 3.2	.1	1.3
		+ New long-term debt or stock		12.0	−	−	−	−
		+ Increase (decrease) in additional short-term debt and notes payable (existing)		2.5	1.0	3.2	− .1	− 1.3
		Change in cash and marketable securities		**− .1**	**0**	**0**	**0**	**0**
Borrowing base analysis		Borrowing base‡		$ 28.7	$ 26.7	$ 23.8	$ 23.2	$ 22.1
		− Required indebtedness§		27.4	25.1	24.8	21.3	16.6
		Excess (deficient) borrowing base		**1.3**	**1.6**	**− 1.0**	**1.9**	**5.5**

*Columns may not add up to totals because of rounding.

†Except cash and marketable securities, notes payable (existing), additional short-term debt, and current maturities of long-term debt.

‡Calculated using year-end balance sheet values: 80% of accounts receivable plus 50% of inventory plus 50% of net fixed assets.

§The total required borrowings at year-end: current maturities of long-term debt plus notes payable (existing) plus additional short-term debt plus long-term debt.

LIVERPOOL JOHN MOORES UNIVERSITY

No. 968128

Self Collection of holds

Last 6 digits of barcode no. located on the bottom of your University card

Please issue the item at the self service machine before you leave this area.

ljmu.ac.uk | LIBRARY SERVICES

Four questions

Acme's management must now assess the impact of this worst case scenario on the company's solvency. Does the company have enough staying power to get through the bad years of 1987 and 1988 without a creditor-initiated legal action? Four questions must be answered.

Do we need external financing to get through the bad period? The best outcome, of course, would be to generate enough cash from internal sources to service debt and cover the losses during the downturn. Some companies with floundering projects may be able to do this if: (1) the company is not highly leveraged; (2) the project, while large in absolute dollar terms, is small relative to the company's size; or (3) the project's cash flows are inversely correlated with the cash flows of the base business so that if the project goes bad, the base business can still generate enough cash. Under such circumstances, the company does not have to seek external financing or request deferrals of principal payments. This position indicates a high degree of staying power and suggests that the project does not create excessive risk.

The additional short-term debt line on the balance sheet (as shown in *Exhibit II*) tells the story. It is the forecasting "plug number" that makes the balance sheet balance. The number rises when the company operates at a cash flow deficit and must obtain external debt financing. It falls when the company generates surplus cash and repays the debt. In Acme's case, the figure takes a big jump to $2.5 million in 1986, a profitable year, because the company must boost its current assets to support the new sales the plant expansion generates. The company obtains this amount by drawing under its line of credit, which would then be fully used.

Then in 1987 and 1988, the problem years, the company needs $4.2 million more in short-term borrowings because of the losses and the repayment of long-term debt. Thus if the worst case scenario came to pass, Acme would have to get the bank's assistance.

Do lenders have to supply any "net new money"? Banks and other lenders are more willing to work with a troubled borrower if they do not have to raise their risk exposure. Provided that the company has minimal collateral coverage—one dollar of borrowing base for each dollar loaned—they view their existing loans as spilled milk that they hope eventually to recover from cash flow after the borrower has returned to profitability. Under such circumstances, lenders will usually advance funds to make payments on other debts owed to them or, more likely, defer the payments.

But if a forecast shows that, in spite of attempts to conserve cash, the company must still seek net new financing, then the risks may appear too high. Banks and other lenders do not see themselves as suppliers of money to finance losses; equity capital does that. Nor do they like to advance money to a severely troubled company so that it can repay other lenders.

While bankers will occasionally advance limited amounts of new funds, forecasters are foolish to presume that the bank will be willing to raise its loss exposure. The conservative forecaster should not expect to get net new money unless the company has a legally binding revolving credit commitment and the forecast shows that no restrictive covenants would be broken that would permit the bank to cancel the commitment. Draws should be assumed under a nonlegally binding line of credit only during the first year of a problem period because these credits are renewable at yearly intervals at the bank's option. The draws should be covered at least one-to-one by the borrowing base since the bank, which is only morally bound under a line of credit, could refuse the draw requests unless the company has collateral coverage.

Acme borrows from one bank, so even though additional short-term debt rises in 1987 and 1988, the decline in required indebtedness (shown at the bottom of *Exhibit II*) means that the short-term bank loans merely furnish the cash to repay the bank's long-term debt on time. Thus the bank does not have to supply any net new money. In reality, the bank would probably defer the principal payments on the long-term debt. Its willingness to support Acme will depend on Acme's having minimal collateral coverage.

Can the company stay in compliance with its borrowing base? At the bottom of *Exhibit II* is the borrowing base analysis, which shows how much debt Acme's assets will support. The analysis shows that the company lacks the staying power to survive. It would need to incur maximum borrowings (required indebtedness) in 1988 of $24.8 million, but it can only support debt of $23.8 million. Thus if Acme implements the large-scale expansion and encounters very hard times, it could not count on lender support when debts and other obligations come due. Acme could face an involuntary bankruptcy or other legal action. It should, therefore, reject this expansion option as too risky.

What are the costs of lender assistance? Lender assistance may take several forms depending on the situation: loans under existing credit commitments, deferrals of principal payments, or advances of new money outside existing commitments. At the

---

Exhibit III   **Assessing staying power**

Borrowing base coverage

Result of balance sheet forecast during problem years	High	Low	Negative
No additional short-term debt (ASTD) needed	Sufficient	Sufficient	Sufficient
ASTD needed but available under existing credit commitments	Sufficient	Sufficient	Sufficient
ASTD needed but it represents principal deferrals on existing debt	Sufficient	Sufficient	Insufficient
ASTD needed and it represents net new money to a lender	Probably insufficient	Insufficient	Insufficient

Staying power: Sufficient / Probably insufficient / Insufficient

---

least, the costs of this assistance will include tougher loan terms:

A pledge of collateral if loans are unsecured or additional collateral if they are already secured.

Guarantees of repayment by subsidiaries.

The owners' personal guarantees if the company is privately held.

New covenants that tightly control or eliminate various cash drains: dividend payments, capital expenditures, and outside investments.

An interest rate increase.

In addition to these changes in loan terms, as a lender's risk of loss grows, it will usually pressure management or the board of directors to reduce expenses (that is, cut head count) and sell assets to generate cash, seek a buyer for the company, or replace management.

The following guidelines will help managers gauge the costs of lender assistance:

☐ Demands for more stringent loan terms start if company losses persist past three or four quarters, especially if the company violates a restrictive covenant in a loan agreement. But a high borrowing base coverage will postpone or minimize these demands.

☐ Regardless of borrowing base coverage, if losses continue more than two years, lender demands will be heard, and unless coverage is high, the lender will apply some pressure.

☐ If principal deferrals are necessary, expect the full range of demands and expect pressure to be brought to bear. If the borrowing base coverage is low or losses are large, the resulting pressure can be intense.

□   When the company's committed credit facilities are fully used and it still needs new money, the lender may exert intense pressures and deny the loan requests. Such denials will usually lead to a default on one or more obligations.

Acme did a staying power analysis on phase one of the $6.5 million small-scale expansion. Additional short-term debt would be necessary in 1987 and 1988. Even though earnings were considerably less than in the large-scale option, since less debt had to be repaid, the company had an adequate borrowing base to survive the recession. The total borrowing requirement was $18.6 million in 1988; it was narrowly covered by a borrowing base of $19.5 million. Acme would need additional short-term debt in 1987 and 1988 to repay existing long-term bank debt, that is, a principal deferral. In exchange for this assistance, management should expect intense demands and pressures since the losses would be long lasting and the borrowing base coverage would be low.

The decision

The type of lender assistance, if any, needed during the problem years plus the borrowing base coverage tell whether a capital-spending program would leave the company with enough staying power to avoid creditors calling a default and demanding payment during hard times. *Exhibit III* shows how to determine if a company has enough staying power.

Going ahead with a project that has insufficient staying power means risking the entire company. Even if the analysis reveals sufficient staying power, management still needs to consider:

The likelihood of the worst case scenario becoming a reality.

The costs of any needed lender assistance.

Management's attitude toward outside interference.

The strategic necessity of the investment.

The potential profitability of the investment.

Since Acme's survival would not be at risk, management might well accept the small-scale

option with the intention of embarking on phase two in a year if things go as planned.

A short aside: a company with publicly held bonds usually has less staying power than a company that relies on bank debt and privately placed bonds. If we change the Acme example and assume that the long-term debt was in the form of public bonds, then Acme's bank would have to loan the additional short-term debt that results in the analysis of the small-scale option because arranging principal deferrals on publicly held debt is extremely difficult. Thus Acme's bank would be called on to supply substantial net new money, and it would probably refuse because of the low borrowing base coverage. The conclusion of the analysis would change: the $6.5 million small-scale project is also too risky.

In the late summer of 1981, an oil-field supply company I handled made a large loan request. As part of my due diligence work, I made a telephone survey of executives at some 20 companies involved in various aspects of the energy business to obtain their forecast of drilling activity. The people I called were high-ranking officials at major oil companies, drilling contractors, and large oil-field equipment manufacturers. Virtually every one said that drilling would remain strong for two to five years. I made these calls less than six months before the boom ended.

This incident illustrates how wrong bright and experienced businesspeople can be about their companies' and industries' future. No matter how convinced managers may be of a capital expenditure program's profit potential or strategic necessity, they should take a hard look at the project's downside to make sure the company does not assume an imprudent amount of risk. Staying power analysis is a good way to do this. ⊖

Implementation

If we are to grow as advanced technology grows,
we must realize the new importance of . . .

THE PROJECT MANAGER

By Paul O. Gaddis

In new and expanding fields like electronics, nucleonics, astronautics, avionics, and cryogenics, a new type of manager is being bred. Although he goes by many titles, the one most generally used is *project manager*. His role in modern industry deserves more scrutiny than it has received from students of management and professional managers.

Generally speaking, the project manager's business is to create a *product* — a piece of advanced-technology hardware. The primary tool available to him is the brainpower of men who are professional specialists in diverse fields. He uses this tool in all the phases of the creation of his product, from concept through the initial test operation and manufacturing stages.

This article will consider those functions of management which receive special emphasis in advanced-technology industry:

- What does a project manager in advanced-technology industry do?
- What kind of man must he be?
- What training is prerequisite for success?

Before going into these topics, let us first take a look at this new industry in which the project manager works.

Meeting Specifications

Advanced-technology industry is the kind of business where a complex product is designed, developed, and manufactured to meet predetermined performance specifications. The advanced-technology company is committed at the outset to succeed in meeting these performance specifications or acceptable modifications thereof.

In this kind of work the development phase is always substantial, since the essential function of the new industry is the adaptation of recent research findings to the solution of specific problems in creating a new product. But operating groups in advanced-technology companies do not themselves perform fundamental research. While advanced-technology practitioners recognize the essential need for a vital output of fundamental research, and are in fact dependent on this output for survival as an industry, they do not work in the fundamental areas.

Unit Organization

A project is an organization unit dedicated to the attainment of a goal — generally the successful completion of a developmental product on time, within budget, and in conformance with predetermined performance specifications.

The project staff will be a "mix" of brainpower, varying with the project's mission. For example, a project involving a high degree of development, such as one devoted to achieving a practical demonstration of ionic propulsion that can later be applied in rocketry, will have a high proportion of scientists to engineers and a high proportion of theoretically inclined personnel. In contrast, a project committed to attaining a successful full-power trial of a propulsion engine utilizing a proven solid propellant will have more engineers than scientists.

Projects are typically organized by task (vertical structure) instead of by function (horizontal organization). The relative advantages of "project" and "systems" organizations have been the subject of widespread controversy, and it is not my intent here to elaborate on this issue. The obvious organizational goal is to seek the advantages of both — the vertical structure in which the control and performance associated with autonomous management are maintained for a given project, and the horizontal in which better continuity, flexibility, and use of scarce talents may be achieved in a technical group.

Unique Characteristics

A study of the project manager function must examine these topics: what he does, what he must be, and what training he needs. In considering these, I shall limit myself to the more or less autonomous project in which "real" management and personnel responsibility resides with the project manager. This autonomy is in contrast to the organization in which the project function is maintained by a "project engineer," who often is relegated to a staff position with responsibilities far outweighing his authority, and who must pursue tenuous relationships with a great deal of skill and persistence to achieve even modest performance goals.

Different Approach

How does the job of the advanced-technology project manager differ from the picture of the conventional manager in modern industry? For one thing, he is managing a higher proportion of *professionals*, from the working level of the "journeyman engineer" up through his subordinate managers. Even in manufacturing operations on advanced-technology products it is often necessary to introduce engineers and scientists to the laboratory floor in large numbers. As further evidence of the technological infiltration, note that purchasing groups for these projects are likely to be staffed by a substantial proportion of engineers.

In view of this, the project manager needs a different attitude regarding the classic management functions of control, coordination, communication, and the setting of performance standards. Moreover, the professional attitude and approach is steadily gaining emphasis and more widespread acceptance throughout all of the engineering industries.

In learning to manage a group of professional employees, the usual boss-subordinate relationship must be modified. Of especial importance, the *how* — the details or methods of work performance by a professional employee — should be established *by the employee*. It follows that he must be given the facts necessary to permit him to develop a rational understanding of the *why* of tasks assigned to him.

Moreover, if this kind of employee is to be treated as a professional, he must have established for him performance standards of the highest order, and must be accountable for productivity at the professional level. He may be granted the prerogatives of a professional — independence of detailed supervision, freedom from administrative routine where feasible, and working quarters which afford privacy and comfort. But at the same time he must never be excused from the responsibility of having to *produce* in accordance with the exacting requirements of his profession.

These points are illustrated by the actions of a line engineer in a West Coast company:

This manager had cut his teeth on the air-frame assembly lines, but was now leading a group which was assembling and checking out highly complex air-borne electronics equipment. He decided that there was a real need in his group for a young electronics engineer who would assist in the interpretation of quality control tests.

After obtaining the necessary approval from management, he made several requests to the "professional employment office" to get such an engineer.

Following about two weeks of waiting, however, he saw that there seemed to be no intention to start action on his behalf in the personnel office. In exasperation, he finally called on the supervisor of professional employment, who was a doctor of engineering placed in this position to expedite the acquisition of key scientific personnel. The manager was told somewhat blandly by the young academician that the employment office had never been informed of the *reasons* why an assembly and test group should require the services of an additional professional electronics engineer.

After the manager had finished sputtering about line authority not needing reasons, he finally came to realize that his best course of action would be to explain in painful detail his need for the additional engineer. The supervisor accepted his reasons, and he got his new engineer in a week.

"Blind Flying"

Another unique aspect of the project manager's job is that his task is finite in duration. He cannot see a reasonably long line of repetitive or similar functions stretching ahead of him as his management counterparts in manufacturing or sales do. Nor can he modify his assembly line to manufacture a new product. He is managing a specific group of advanced specialists; the professional mix of his group is tailored specifically for the accomplishment of an assigned mission. If he and his group are successful performers, they will complete all facets of their job, and so work themselves out of a job, as quickly as possible. This may be a year or less in some projects, and may run to five years and upward for long-range, high-budget projects.

In any case, the project manager must trust his corporate management, implicitly in most cases, to provide him and his forces with continuity of work on successive projects. Needless to say, the record of top management in achieving this continuity will affect the peace of mind, if not the performance, of the project manager and his entire staff.

Another feature of the project manager's job is the absence of feedback information during the early stages and often other stages of his project. Under the servomechanism analogy of management control, a manager establishes a closed loop in which the performance output of his group is fed back to him, compared with performance standards, and corrective control action is then directed into the system.

However, in advanced-technology work, during the design phase of a project and before test results of newly developed equipment are available, the project manager often finds himself like a pilot flying blind, assisted by a relatively unproven set of instruments. His experience, judgment, and faith must carry him through until early test results become available; from this first feedback he can modify the design approach in a direction most likely to meet the acid requirements of further proof tests. Meanwhile, during these periods of blind flying, he may be forced to make long-term decisions which commit substantial funds.

Taking Risks

It is because of these "facts of life" in project work that crisis, uncertainty, and suspense are continually recurring to test the mettle of the manager and his staff. To illustrate:

A project group was developing a small liquid fuel missile for a military mission. Early in the project it became apparent that a new high-capacity pump for the propulsion system was going to be needed.

After an exhaustive analysis of the problem, it was decided that the prospects for developing and proving the kind of pump needed, in the time interval permitted by the project schedule, were good enough to warrant committing the project to the use of this pump.

A pump vendor was selected, and this vendor in turn set up his own subproject under a rigorous time schedule to develop the new pump in time

for the missile application. As a matter of prudence an alternate pump supplier was also charged with the mission of producing a pump to meet the requirements, using a different design approach from that of the first supplier.

During the months which ensued, the responsibility for the validity of the initial decision never rested lightly on the management personnel in the project. In the normal course of progress, substantial funds were committed to the propulsion system design and to the procurement of other components for the system. Moreover, it was at times necessary to make partly intuitive decisions based on the engineers' progress on the pump under development. These decisions in turn affected the design of the other components in the system.

For a period of five months, the entire progress in design and procurement of hardware was based on faith in the integrity of the original pump decision. This foundation became more substantial only when one of the two pump suppliers was able to place a prototype of his pump in a test loop and prove its performance. And even here there was risk, since many new components have worked beautifully in the prototype test stage but have been subject to failures when the manufactured versions were placed in use.

One of the two developmental pumps proved clearly unsuccessful, while the other just barely met performance requirements on the test stand. This necessitated a vigorous redesign effort in the project. The pump performance specifications were somewhat relaxed, and the remainder of the system was altered to accommodate the new piece of equipment. Late changes had to be accepted, both on the drawing boards and in the shops, in the other components being procured for the system. In short, the project staff went through a period of technological "crisis." In this case, fortunately, the crisis was successfully resolved. The project's prototype missile was ready for test with only a minor delay in schedule.

Authority & Responsibility

Essential to the project management concept is a clear delineation of authority and responsibility. The manager knows that his basic responsibilities are to deliver his end product (1) in accordance with performance requirements, (2) within the limitations of his budget, and (3) within the time schedule that his company or customer has specified. In general, the manager will delegate by tasks, so that subordinate managers in his group will have these same three responsibilities for subprojects.

Success or failure may well hinge on the

manager's ability to discern fine variations in emphasis among performance, budget, and time schedule needs and to resolve the continuous apparent conflicts which occur between them. During the life of an average project the relative importance of each of his three responsibilities may change several times. It can be fatal to overemphasize the schedule when dollars have become the governing requirement, or vice versa. Likewise, performance requirements must be met or trimmed to fit reality. The skillful project manager will aim for a balanced emphasis; he will try to stay flexible so he can shift and adapt to new circumstances as they occur.

Keeping Things Moving

Like the line manager, the project manager is at once a man of action, a man of thought, and a front man. As a man of action, his most important function will be the establishment and the preservation of a sense of momentum throughout all layers of his project. What he will strive hardest to avoid is "dead center" situations in which general inertia seems to become overpowering and his technical people for the moment see no direction in which to advance. Thus, the usual management function of trouble shooting, or of unraveling the knots, will occupy a great deal of his time.

The first-line supervisors — the "supervising engineers" — are by definition the men who play the key roles in guiding the day-by-day progress of a project toward its goals. Such a supervisor often bears the same range of burdens borne by his manufacturing counterpart; demands on his time can easily be overpowering if the project manager does not act to shield him from diversionary requirements.

At the same time it should be borne in mind that in attempting to shield a supervisor, to free him to concentrate chiefly on the vital engineering job at hand, the project manager can unknowingly deal a severe blow to the supervisor's advancement potential. The supervisor is at a critical point in his career, at which leadership capability and administrative potential can blossom or be blighted. A general and basic tenet of management — the training of individuals for leadership — must not be shelved merely because the pace of an advanced-technology project seems at times to be overpowering. Instead the project manager must walk the middle course. For example, he may shield the supervisor from poorly founded requests for detailed information by a staff office, while at the same time letting him resolve with the personnel department a tough question in personnel administration involving one of his engineers.

Dealing With Perfectionists

In pursuing his objective of maintaining momentum, the project manager must be constantly aware of the apparent disdain for time commitments which prevails on the part of the more theoretically inclined scientists and engineers. While this attitude is a rather deep study in itself, one part of it that must be understood is the drive for perfection that so often characterizes the professional mind. Any kind of promised delivery date inevitably involves a compromise with perfection, in that the product or study must be cut off, wrapped up, and delivered at that point, thereby leaving dangling the further improvements which the scientist would like to make. The tendency to finish the job to a T, if allowed to run rampant, can result in continuous postponements of output and reduce the productivity of the project as a whole.

In the nuclear power industry, one can find in almost any reactor project a common example of the perfectionist and his tribulations:

A nuclear reactor core — representing an investment of hundreds of thousands of dollars — must be loaded with a specific amount of fissionable fuel (usually uranium). The decision of just how much fuel is correct is one of the more agonizing which must be faced by industry technologists.

Typically, the loading is set by the designers using early calculations based on a series of simplified reactor experiments with varying quantities of nuclear fuel. While this first loading figure is adequate, it varies from the *optimum* depending on the performance of the nuclear designers in their highly complex and difficult art. Nevertheless, the prolonged processes of reactor core manufacture must be commenced without further delay, and during the ensuing year or longer the scientists undertake a detailed performance analysis of the reactor core with the established loading. This analysis is conducted by means of the most advanced high-capacity digital computers, and hopefully yields a confirmation of the fuel loading. Specifically it tells the designers how close they have come to the optimum loading; the nearer the optimum, the greater the reliability of the reactor, and the more economic its performance.

The perfectionist problem first arises when preliminary information about the fuel loading is requested by the manufacturing engineers from the designers. The nuclear designers are reluctant to part with what they feel are "premature" data. From this point on, the project manager faces a tough series of decisions — he will have to balance the demands of the schedule with the incremental improvements in data to be gained by continuing the design study "one more week." The designers will be quite articulate in expressing the gains to be realized by deferring the schedule.

In every nuclear project the time must come when, by management decree if necessary, the first loading data are released and further improvement is considered unwarranted. At this point the manufacturing engineers commence to build the reactor, while the scientists begin the detailed, confirmatory analysis of the reactor they have just designed. In the nuclear industry, fortunately, the detailed analysis generally confirms that the originally established loading was near optimum, thanks largely to the very high caliber of scientists and engineers in this field.

Organization Planning

In addition to his everyday job of keeping the work moving, the project manager should put a good deal of thought into planning. The crux of effective performance of any project lies in the interrelationship between organizational structure and individuals. The art of organization planning involves the correct tailoring of organizational structure to available individuals, and vice versa. An often-repeated thought in the literature of scientific administration is that although the organizational structure of a project is important, if not vital, it will not make up for inadequate caliber of technologists in the organization. On the other hand, poor organization structure can tie up the output of top-notch engineers and scientists.

In advanced-technology industries, sound organization planning requires adroitness in recruiting scarce talent both from within and without the parent organization. It also involves the ability to utilize engineers and scientists who in some cases do not measure up to reasonable requirements for the project — the ability to shape a team which can "play over its head" when it has to. Sound organization planning in a project cannot be done without a thorough understanding of the personalities, the characteristics, and the attitudes of all the technologists, both as individuals and as members of their particular professional methodologies.

Heading Off

Advance planning is vital in a project. In this area, an important duty of the project man-

ager is to avoid the crises that often manifest themselves during the design, manufacturing, and checkout stages. Perfection will never be attained, and the best efforts of the manager can serve only to reduce, never to eliminate, these crises. Still, advance planning pays for itself many times over.

While technological crises have become accepted as an inherent part of our advanced-technology projects, it must always be realized that each of these crucial periods leaves residual effects throughout the remaining course of the project. Thus, the resolution of such a crisis generally involves a sacrifice of engineering principle for expediency, which may in turn lead to subsequent crises. Further, each crisis, with its resultant need for immediate solution, erodes the constructive attitude of the project's engineers and scientists, particularly the theoreticians.

Clearly, therefore, the more that can be done to avoid or alleviate these situations in advance, the better. It is unfortunately true that *most* crises that arise during the course of a project can be traced to lack of adequate advance planning.

Selling & Reselling

At any time during the course of the project, the manager may be called on to act as front man to help shape or reshape the policies that affect his project relative to the corporate structure and the company's development objectives. Contrary to much opinion about the advanced-technology industries, "selling" is a never-ending job of a project manager, as it is of most other senior managers in the corporate organization. In the matters of acquiring scarce funds, people, and materials, the project manager must always be able to make an effective presentation, often on short notice. Many project managers have suddenly found themselves, in mid-course, fighting for the very existence of their project.

While the outcome of many such struggles is often beyond the influence of any actions taken by the manager, it is true that in numerous other cases his actions as a fully informed representative of the project will have a profound influence on the outcome.

Man in Between

As the foregoing may suggest, life is not dull for a project manager. He is the man in between management and the technologist — the one man in the organization who must be at home in the front office talking about budgets, time schedules, and corporate policies *and* at home in the laboratory talking about technical research and development problems. But he is not a superman. He cannot be expected to double as a member of the executive committee and as a scientist equally well. Being a little of both, he is different from both — and it is precisely this quality which makes him so valuable. In his own right he does what neither the front-office executive nor the scientist can do: accomplish the aims of his corporate management, while serving as a perpetual buffer so that the engineers and scientists can meet the technological objectives that only they can define and only their output can meet.

Clearly, therefore, the job is an unusual one. What manner of man is needed to fill it? What aptitudes should he have? What special difficulties should he be willing and able to handle?

Reasonable "Projectitis"

The subject of "projectitis" may appropriately be examined here; it is a seeing of all things as though a particular project were the center of the corporate universe — the alpha and the omega of the development effort. This phenomenon of organizational beings as observed in World War II was called "theateritis." The late General Henry H. Arnold, in his autobiography *Global Mission*,[1] remarked that the disease of theateritis — the inability of an Air Force commander to be cognizant of the problems of war in any theater other than his own — caused him great concern and trouble in his personal dealings with his top field commanders. However, General Arnold noted at the same time that he would not have under his command any general who did not suffer from this disease.

The project manager on his own battleground needs a modicum of "projectitis" to generate the necessary drive and momentum to spark the project to success. These symptoms of projectitis will be observed by top corporate executives, but they will expect this malady and will themselves suffer with acute outbreaks from time to time, depending on which and how many of their projects are in the limelight.

However, when dealing with his engineers and scientists, the project manager must not suffer, or appear to suffer, from any blind or extreme case of projectitis in establishing sched-

ular aims and policy objectives. If he does succumb to this tendency, perhaps as a result of pressure from an afflicted management, at least two adverse results may occur: (1) technological advancement in the development of his product, which in actuality is the most basic of the project's responsibilities, will suffer; (2) the human resources of the project (the most important resources in advanced-technology industry) will be reduced in efficiency and productivity.

Free Communication

The subject of communication deserves much attention in project management, just as in all management.

The theoretically inclined technologist, generally a man of imaginative creativity, as well, often, as his engineering brother with the more factual kind of creativity, inherently regards the right to communicate as the bread of life for an adequate scientific career. To this principle is related the cherished right to publish scientific work for the judgment of one's scientific peers.

Yet there is a contradictory element in the attitude of scientists toward communication. It may be suspected, based on observations in any professional technological group, that there are some who pay only lip service to the ideal of free communication and who in reality are more than hesitant in communicating the results of their work, or their attitudes on any topic, to anyone connected with administration.

Vannevar Bush, in his book *Modern Arms and Free Men*,[2] noted the distinctly different reactions to communication which he observed among military men and academicians:

❧ In the military there is vigorous and open debate on proposed actions before the decision. But when an office with clearly constituted authority makes the decision, the antagonists, acting under a basic doctrine of their profession, swing around to support actively the idea they had opposed.

❧ In contrast, under the customs which prevail in academic circles, the duly established decision signals the start of the fight. In this environment, it is very difficult to learn the nature of the opposition to administrative planning, since academicians are not inclined to communicate freely in such matters. Consequently, after decisions are drawn there tends to be considerable passive and sometimes active resistance in the execution of the ideas.

The lessons here for the project manager are plain. He must expend considerable active ef-

[1] New York, Harper & Brothers, 1949.

[2] New York, Simon and Schuster, Inc., 1949.

fort in learning to communicate adequately with his scientists and in developing the communicative attitudes of his engineers. It has been clearly demonstrated that scientists and engineers who work in the operating environment *can* adapt their output to mesh with corporate schedules and budgets, if they are *adequately informed* regarding corporate policies and objectives. Budgets and schedules must not be mere edicts, but should be carefully prepared with the cognizance of and with the aid of the technologists who must live by them. Whenever occasional arbitrary actions originate in the realms of policy, they should be explained as carefully as possible, and on this basis they will be accepted and implemented.

The Next Project

The temporal aspect of a project manager's task may strain his capacities in dealing with people. Because the duration of a project is well defined, it is only human for the scientists and engineers who work on it to come to anticipate their next assignment, even though it may be a year or more away. This can result in a kind of divided allegiance, in which the engineers look to others outside the project who may be able to help them in gaining their next assignment.

The project manager must counter this tendency to cast about for the next task, for it will diminish his effective control of the present task. In this effort he must be bulwarked by a potent company sales policy that has provided and will continue to provide new projects for professional employees. When he has this backing, the manager then need only follow a basic rule of managerial conduct — that of letting his people know where they stand. Frankness and integrity, when used in discussing the future, will allay their instinctive concern about the job that is over the horizon. It will convince them their role in future projects is assured unless they have been told otherwise.

Qualifications for Success

Some of the qualifications that a successful project manager must possess proceed logically from the preceding discussion:

(1) His career must have been molded in the advanced-technology environment.

(2) He must have a working knowledge of many fields of science, the fundamental kind of knowledge which he can augment when necessary to delve into the intricacies of a specific technology.

(3) He must have a good understanding of general management problems — especially marketing, control, contract work, purchasing, law, and personnel administration. The concept of *profitability* should be familiar to him.

(4) He must have a strong, continuous, active interest in teaching, training, and developing his supervisors.

In reviewing these qualifications, one can observe the emphasis on the *integrative* function in the operations of the project manager. There is an ever-present requirement for the joining of many parts into a systematic whole. Describing the processes by which the integrative mind works is, of course, difficult, for they are largely indefinable, just as the requisite qualities for managerial personnel are not subject to scientific definition. It is clear, however, that the integrative mind must deal with intangible factors as well as the tangible, and that there is need also at times for an intuitive process in the formulation of judgment and decision (especially where men's reactions are an important factor). It is perhaps in this respect that the outlook of a good project manager differs most sharply from that of the researcher:

The methodology of scientific analysis and experimentation has been carefully developed over many years and is a part of the indoctrination of young men in training for a scientific career. This indoctrination breeds a distrust of intuition and a tendency to disregard intangibles. Further, the analytical mind will not draw its hypothesis until all relevant data have been observed and interpreted. If a hypothesis must be drawn before this, it must be thoroughly qualified and hedged in the interests of scientific accuracy.

In project organizations, it is recognized that the analytical mind produces the concepts by which the project advances toward its goal. But without the integrative function, often nothing would be done with the concepts originating in the analytical function. The topnotch manager of an advanced-technology project must be capable of both integration and analysis, and must understand that the rigorous training of professional technologists with its emphasis on analysis sometimes impairs their integrative ability.

Friendly Differences

In discussing the attributes of the project manager, it soon becomes apparent that he has much in common with his corporate brethren in research administration. The research director also works in advanced technologies and holds similar responsibilities. His usual task is to lead research groups in planning and developing new products which will fit into his company's future marketing plans.

Tactics vs. Strategy

However, there are subtle, yet substantive, differences in the managerial approach of the advanced-technology project manager and that of the research administrator. In military parlance, the former is primarily a tactician, the latter essentially a strategist.

These differences may be illustrated by a look at the typical kinds of meetings in which these two managers are likely to be engaged:

◖ For the project manager, it is a clutch meeting with officials of a key supplier — a meeting which is the result of previous efforts falling short of their goals. The chief engineer and the manufacturing superintendent of the supplier firm are present, well primed with absolute reasons why they cannot make scheduled delivery of a critical piece of hardware, without which the project manager cannot complete his product.

After the opening formalities are over, this meeting begins to resemble a kind of combat. The enemy is inertia. There is a persevering, chips-down type of resourcefulness on the part of the project representatives. They must cross-examine all of the advocates who say that the key component cannot be made — the supplier's designers who say the design cannot be completed as intended, or the accountant who says it cannot be built for anywhere near the original cost estimate, or the manufacturing engineer who says it cannot be built the way the denizens of the ivory tower designed it. Then these reasons must be refuted, or if they stand up under this scrutiny, the project's designs must be altered to accommodate a simpler component. In *some* way the project must acquire a usable component, and the threatened loss of schedule or budget must be recouped.

◖ The research administrator's first meeting may be with a budget committee. The controller proclaims that while he can measure the input to the new research program well enough in terms of its cost, he cannot measure the output very well at all (and really is it worthwhile anyway?).

The second meeting is with a marketing committee. The sales manager states that he cannot understand why a certain research group after two years has not produced the widget which he is sure will revolutionize the market.

The third meeting is with a staff committee,

where the research manager is straining to acquaint policy people wtih the company's technical problems so that they may appreciate the broad implications of these problems.

Both these roles require resourcefulness. It might be said, however, that the project manager's task requires an *intensive* resourcefulness, in which his efforts are ever directed against obstacles to progress. Conversely, the research administrator must display an *extensive* resourcefulness in meeting his primary objective — i.e., supplying his company with enough new products, and at the right time, to protect its market position against the competitive forces of product obsolescence. This requires him to handle some tough intangibles: How do you measure the output of a research group, or its impact on the company's market position? How do you evaluate the feasibility and potential payoff of new product concepts?

The project manager, in his tactical role, is closely related to line-operating management. In the research administrator's strategic role, there are many elements of the key staff adviser's functions, as well as the requirement for leading engineers and scientists in a research program. This program generally represents a wider road, traveled under less exigent circumstances, than the narrow road and fast pace followed by the advanced-technology project.

Reporting Progress

A further insight into the differences between these two types of managers may be gained by considering the way that status accounting is handled. Enlightened research administration has generally learned that it is unwise to burden a research team by requiring from it regular status reports on a periodic basis. Rather, it is preferable to require the team to submit a report only when it has something to report, since research advances do not come by regular increments of the calendar.

However, in the advanced-technology project, periodic status reports are appropriate and valuable. A report showing the absence of advance during a reporting period is an important indicator of trouble to project management.

Thinkers & Doers

Before the Sputnik era, William H. Whyte, Jr., leveled a very penetrating criticism against attempts to make scientists conform to the organization in U.S. industry.[3] Since the Sputniks, others have jumped on this rolling band wagon and have generated an impressive indictment of the smothering of individuality and inhibition of creativity resulting from the integration of scientists and engineers with organized corporate groups.

While most of this criticism has validity, it should not be interpreted to reflect adversely on the project method of getting advanced-technology results. Project people know and understand that basic and fundamental research is being slighted in this country; they realize that project staffs — the doers — will run out of work to do unless the storehouse of basic scientific knowledge is effectively and continuously replenished. They are also keenly aware that the laissez-faire environment, the unorganized structure, of the world's great laboratories has been the origin of technological advancement.

Using Lab Output

The project method has proved to be an effective way of *utilizing* the scientific output of the thinkers in the laboratories. The project — i.e., group, organization, team, task force, or whatever name it may go by — has piled up a fine record of accomplishment since the days of the famed Manhattan Project. Certainly there has been a requirement of conformity; and, usually, little latitude has been allowed the scientists and engineers in determining the areas in which they will work or the subject which they will investigate, because of requirements for interlocking efforts on a large scale. Yet the records of achievement remain.

For those men with the mental and personal endowment for the project kind of work — the men of factual creativity, the applied scientists, the practicing technologists — there is no element of professional degradation in this work. On the contrary, this type of professional finds the project pace challenging and exhilarating, as can be easily verified by observation — and far preferable to the apparent aimlessness of the pure research environment.

Two Streams of Knowledge

The real indictment of the organization can come only when professional technologists are

[3] *The Organization Man* (New York, Simon and Schuster, Inc., 1956), Part V, "The Organization Scientist."

misused, when the group tries to fit the square peg into the round hole. Those scientists who are genuinely creative, and who can justifiably exhibit the individualism of a fundamental researcher, are rare. It is a shameful waste to attempt to use such men in a project — a waste to the nation, in that their output is hobbled and misapplied, and a loss to the project effort, in that they probably will not contribute to its progress.

Discerning men have long observed that "project people" are inspired by more immediate, if less exalted, goals. In the words of Francis Bacon, penned about 1620 in the preface to his *Novum Organum*:

"Let there be therefore (and may it be for the benefit of both) two streams and two dispensations of knowledge; and in like manner two tribes or kindreds of students in philosophy — tribes not hostile or alien to each other, but bound together by mutual services . . . let there in short be one method for the cultivation, another for the invention, of knowledge.

"And for those who prefer the former, either from hurry, or from consideration of business, or for want of mental power to take in and embrace the other (which must needs be most men's case), I wish that they may succeed to their desire in what they are about, and obtain what they are pursuing. But if any man there be who, not content to rest in and use the knowledge which has already been discovered, aspires to penetrate further . . . I invite all such to join themselves, as true sons of knowledge, with me, that passing by the outer courts of nature, which numbers have trodden, we may find a way at length into her inner chambers."

Role in the Future

The United States today faces the enormous problem of how to regain undisputed technological leadership. The character of American technological advancement during the next five years will shape our future and determine our survival or extinction.

The role to be played by project management in these years ahead will be challenging, exciting, and crucial. Truly it will be the acid test of the project manager and the project concept, but it will be much more than that. It will be a momentous trial of free enterprise, business administration, and progressive industrial management as we know them today.

Getting Things Done

How to make a team work

Maurice Hardaker and Bryan K. Ward

Anyone who has ever run a business or organized a project has discovered how hard it can be to get the whole team on board to ensure that everyone knows where the enterprise is heading and agrees on what it will take to succeed.

At IBM we've used a method for some years that helps managers do just this. The technique, which we call PQM or Process Quality Management, grew out of many studies with customers to determine their needs and from

In one intense session, managers set goals, accept responsibilities – and become a real team.

internal studies as part of IBM's business quality program. PQM has been used successfully by service companies, government agencies, and nonprofit organizations, as well as manufacturers.

In PQM, managers get back to the often overlooked basics of an endeavor. IBM has had many successes abroad by paying attention to such details.

IBM Europe's manufacturing arm relied heavily on PQM when it

launched a series of changes including continuous-flow manufacturing. First the vice president of manufacturing and his team made sure they understood the task ahead. Then they focused on new priorities for the company's major materials-management processes. As a result of their decisions, changes cascaded through the manufacturing organization's work force, leading not only to better interplant logistics but also to smooth introduction of continuous-flow manufacturing among IBM's 15 European plants. As this happened, manufacturing cycle times and inventory levels improved, costs dropped, quality rose, and the company became more flexible in meeting customer demand. That may not be the end of the rainbow, but it's not bad from a two-day PQM session.

PQM has also been the starting point for many IBM customers of a host of management decisions in such areas as strategy formulation, funding, human resource management, marketing, and resource allocation for large, complex projects. Often a PQM study is undertaken because something has happened – someone sees a new opportunity, a new technology, or new competitors. But it is useful any time.

PQM does not differ radically from other planning processes: we identify goals and the activities critical to their attainment, and we provide a way to measure success. But PQM demands an intensive one- or two-day session at which *all* the key managers

concerned agree on what must be done and accept specific responsibility.

There's no guarantee that a unit will achieve its mission, of course. That requires competent follow-through by the entire organization. But PQM lays the groundwork for such success. And at least all the key players start off facing in the same direction.

Gather the team

PQM begins with a person who is the leader of the management team – the boss, the one whose job depends on getting the team's mission accomplished. He or she should then involve everyone on the immediate management team and no one else – nobody missing and no hitchhikers. At most there should be 12 people, since more than that is just too unwieldy. And if even one member of the team cannot attend the study, wait. PQM requires a buy-in from everyone not only to identify what is needed but also to commit to the process.

By management team we usually mean a formal group of managers, a board of directors, say, or a divisional vice president and his or her top managers. But the team can also be a collection of individuals drawn from various sectors of the company for a specific project, like the team brought together at IBM to introduce continuous-flow manufacturing. In either case, the mission is normally too large or complex for one person, so the boss collects or inherits a team to work on it.

Maurice Hardaker is a senior consultant with IBM's International Education Centre in La Hulpe, Belgium. He has advised the boards of directors of many of IBM's customers. Most recently he has been working with senior management in IBM's program for business process quality management.

Bryan K. Ward is a senior consultant in the Systems Management Consultancy Group of IBM United Kingdom. He advises senior management of IBM customers about business planning and information technology strategy and works with senior management of IBM UK on business-related topics.

PQM demands spontaneity, so even though the boss convokes the team, a neutral outsider should lead the discussions. The leader could be a consultant or a manager or an officer from elsewhere in the company. What's important is that leaders not be the bosses' subordinates and that their livelihood should not depend on achieving the mission. Furthermore, the discussions are best held off premises; at the office, secretaries can fight their way through steel doors to deliver "urgent" messages.

Finally, and perhaps this goes without saying, the boss had better be ready to accept challenges to the status quo. We have presided at a few disasters where, despite assurances of open-mindedness, the boss turned the study into a self-justifying monologue. Fortunately, this is rare; it's a terrible waste of time.

Understand the mission

The first step in the PQM effort is to develop a clear understanding of the team's mission, what its members collectively are paid to do. *Collectively* is important. A marketing vice president and a finance vice president will have different ideas about their separate functional missions. But when they meet together as part of the management team, they should know their jobs as members of that team.

If the mission statement is wrong, everything that follows will be wrong too, so getting a clear understanding is crucial. And agreeing on a mission may not be as easy as it may at first seem. People in well-run companies and government agencies tend to know their job descriptions, the benefits package, and their own job objectives. But even at the top, their ideas about the organization's mission are often pretty vague—to make profits or something like that. In part, this reflects the nature of management teams. People are appointed, stay a while, do their jobs, and move on; each team includes long-serving members, new arrivals, and new leaders. As a group, they may never have articulated their mission to one another. A PQM study makes them stand back and ask fundamental questions like "Do we really

understand our business well enough to form a mission statement?"

Our advice is to make the mission statement explicit—nail it to the wall. It shouldn't be more than

Some managers learn their unit's true mission for the first time.

three or four short sentences. For example, the following is a mission statement for one of IBM Europe's units:

"Prepare IBM World Trade Europe Middle East Africa Corporation employees to establish their businesses.

"Organize high-level seminars for IBM customers and make a significant contribution to IBM's image in Europe.

"Demonstrate the added value of the International Education Centre through excellence in advanced education, internationalism, innovation, and cross-functional exchanges."

The unit's mission statement defines the boundaries of the business (Europe, the Middle East, and Africa) and the customer population (all IBM employees within that area plus senior people from IBM's customers). It says what has to be done and says that achievement will be measured by the unit's demonstrable impact on IBM business successes, customer satisfaction, and company image in Europe.

The mission should be clear enough to let you know when you have succeeded and are entitled to a reward. "Increase profits" is not a rewardable mission. How much of an increase? .5%? 5%? 50%? But "generate positive cash flow" might well be a rewardable mission for a management team nursing a sick company. We did a study with one IBM customer whose mission was quite simply to survive until next year. It had a well-planned strategy for the future but a rough patch to negotiate for the next 12 months.

Once a team has defined its goal or mission, it could go straight to identifying its critical success factors

(CSFs), the things it will have to do to succeed. But in our experience that's premature. At this point, few teams are relaxed enough to do the free associating needed to pinpoint their real CSFs. They are fixed on what they know and on today's problems, not on new possibilities.

To break out of old ways of thinking, we suggest a 10-minute brainstorming session in which team members list one-word descriptions of everything they believe could have an impact on achieving their mission. The usual brainstorming rules should apply:

Everyone should contribute.

Everything is fair game, no matter how crazy or outrageous.

Nobody is permitted to challenge any suggestion.

The facilitator should write everything down so the team can see the whole list.

While thinking about these dominant influences, each member should focus intently on the team's mission. Members should look inside and outside their bailiwicks, sometimes far outside to factors like national characteristics or public policy issues. The dominant influences that turned up in a brainstorming session for a Spanish company, for example, included the socialist government, the Basques, the Catalonians, regionalism, terrorism, and the mañana syndrome. Typically a team's list will contain 30 to 50 diverse items ranging from things like costs and supplier capabilities to jogging and the weather.

Spell out your goals

Now the team should be ready to identify the critical success factors, a term used for many years in corporate planning to mean the most important subgoals of a business, business unit, or project. Here we define CSFs as what the team must accomplish to achieve its mission.

Consensus on these aims is vital. In one study, the top 10 managers in 125 European companies were asked individually to identify their companies' 5 most critical objectives. The minimum number from each company would be 5; the maximum, 50. Managers of the 40 most profitable companies agreed on 6 to 12 objectives. For the 40 worst companies, the range was 26 to 43. In other words, the top executives of the poor performers had no shared vision of what they were trying to do, while just the opposite was true of the successful companies' leaders. Significantly, a few years after the managers of one worst category company had agreed on its critical objectives, the company moved into the most profitable group.[1]

Like the mission, CSFs are not the how to of an enterprise, and they are not directly manageable. Often they are statements of hope or fear. The list in the first part of the *Exhibit* is typical. In a sense, every CSF should be viewed as beginning with the words "We need…" or "We must…" to express buy-in by all ("We") and agreed-on criticality ("need" or "must").

In naming its CSFs, a team should be guided by the necessary-and-sufficient rule. That is, the group must agree that each CSF listed is *necessary* to the mission and that together they are *sufficient* to achieve the mission. This is a stringent requirement. The CSF list must reflect the absolute minimum number of subgoals that have to be achieved for the team to accomplish its mission.

The seven CSFs in the *Exhibit* are designed for a fictitious enterprise that sells consumer products in the United States. It's a mature market, and the company's market share and profitability have eroded. The CEO's mission statement for this business might read:

"Restore market share and profitability over the next two years, and prepare the company and marketplace for further profitable growth."

To accomplish that mission, the management team must achieve all seven CSFs over the next two years. That's what we mean by necessary and sufficient.

In addition, each CSF must be devoted to a single issue—pure in the elemental sense, like hydrogen or gold. The word *and* is verboten. The team has to struggle to reduce its list

honestly; it can't succumb when some creative manager says, "Why don't we combine numbers three and seven so we reduce product cost *and* improve morale?"

The list should be a mix of tactical and strategic factors. If the factors are all strategic (increase market share to 15% by 1992, for example), the business might founder while everybody concentrates on the blue skies ahead. Equally, if all are tactical (reduce the delivered cost of product ABC to $20.50 by year end), the business could kill itself on short-term success. The ratio depends on several considerations, of course, including the nature of the business unit doing the study. A regional sales office would likely have more tactical CSFs, while a corporate headquarters would have an almost entirely strategic list.

The maximum number of CSFs is eight. And if the mission is survival, four is the limit—you don't worry about whether your tie is straight when you are drowning. There is no magic about eight. It just seems to be the largest number of truly critical goals that a management team can focus on continuously.

Our rules on number and absolute consensus may be tough, but they work, and it's essential to follow them. Whenever we have been persuaded to relax either rule, we have ended up with a mess, a list of moans rather than the truly visceral issues affecting the business. If someone cries, "We can't agree, let's vote," don't do it. Insist on consensus; highly paid, experienced, businesswise people should be able to agree on what's vital to their business, after all.

Reaching agreement on the CSFs usually takes from one to three hours. The longest time we've seen was a day. In that case, the team was composed of the heads of nine quasi-independent business units and managers from headquarters. Understandably, they had a tough time reaching consensus.

Find what matters most

The third step in PQM is to identify and list what has to be done so that a company can meet its critical suc-

cess factors. This might mean being more responsive to the market, exploiting new technologies, or whatever else is essential to accomplish the CSFs.

Ask almost any management team for a list of its business activities or processes, however, and you will often get a set of bland descriptions like maintenance or sales or customer service. These aren't business processes. They don't describe what is actually done in the business.

The technique demands unanimity; all must agree to go in the same direction.

We recommend a more rigorous approach, one that draws on our necessary-and-sufficient rule. As with the CSFs' relation to the mission, each process necessary for a given CSF must be indicated, and together all those processes must be sufficient to accomplish it.

Other rules we find useful are:

Each business process description should follow a verb-plus-object sequence.

Every business process should have an owner, the person responsible for carrying out the process.

The owner should be a member of the management team that agreed to the CSFs.

No owner should have more than three or four business processes to manage.

To show how these rules work, think about the process "measure customer satisfaction," listed as P2 in the *Exhibit*. This process has an action verb and an object of the action. It can have an owner, and its quality or performance can be measured. Is this process currently being done? By whom? How often? How well? How well are competitors doing

1 "Strategy and Innovation in the Firm," an unpublished study conducted in 1973 by Charles-Hubert Heyvaert, University of Leuven, Belgium.

Exhibit   Turning a mission into an agenda

Charting a project

Business processes		Critical success factors							Count	Quality
		Best-of-breed product quality	New products that satisfy market needs	Excellent suppliers	Motivated, skilled workers	Excellent customer satisfaction	New business opportunities	Lowest delivered cost		
P1	Research the marketplace								3	C
P2	Measure customer satisfaction								4	D
P3	Advertise products								3	B
P4	Monitor competition								6	D
P5	Measure product quality								5	C
P6	Educate vendors								4	E
P7	Train employees								6	C
P8	Define new product requirements								4	C
P9	Process customer orders								2	B
P10	Develop new products								6	B
P11	Monitor customer complaints								3	D
P12	Negotiate manufacturing designs								5	D
P13	Define future skill needs								3	C
P14	Select and certify vendors								5	C
P15	Promote the company								3	C
P16	Support installed products								3	B
P17	Monitor customer or prospect's business								3	E
P18	Announce new products								3	C

Graphing makes priorities clear

Number of critical success factor impacts

	E	D	C	B	A	
						7
		P4	P7	P10		6
		P12	P5 P14			5
	P6	P2	P8			4
	P17	P11	P1 P18 P13 P15	P3 P16		3
				P9		2
						1
						0

Quality scale

Zone 1

Zone 2

Zone 3

E Embryonic stage

D Bad

C Fair

B Good

A Excellent

P = business process number

it? Since each team member shares collective responsibility for the affected CSFs, the entire team should be interested in the answers. But only one person owns that process—commitment by all, accountability by one.

"Bill customers" is another example of a business process—and it differs a lot from "invoicing," which is

---

In ranking objectives, the team looks beyond what it's doing now to new possibilities.

---

usually the title on the billing-office door. Invoicing is a simple process; bill customers describes a much richer field for disaster. Many functions contribute to billing: sales, field engineering, accounting, legal, distribution, and information services. But the person responsible for the actual invoicing is rarely one who can coordinate all the activities needed to get an accurate, understandable, complete invoice at the right time and at the lowest cost. The invoicing manager isn't likely to have a broad enough view of the business or the power to effect needed change. The result is often customer dissatisfaction, bad cash flow, a lot of arguing and finger pointing, and low morale—in other words, poor competitiveness.

Once identified as an important process, however, billing customers can be assigned to a member of the management team, who will then be responsible for its performance.

Now suppose we have a complete list of important business processes, each of which has an owner. The list is exclusive, since a process has to be important to be there. But it still needs ranking to identify the most critical processes, those whose performance or quality will have the biggest impact on the mission. This is the penultimate stage of our PQM.

First place the processes and the CSFs in random order on a matrix as shown in "Charting a project" in the *Exhibit*. Then focus on the first critical success factor—in our example, "best-

of-breed product quality"—and ask this question: Which business processes must be performed especially well for us to be confident of achieving this CSF? The object is to single out the processes that have a primary impact on this particular CSF. Many business activities will touch on it, of course; what you're after are the essential ones.

The facilitator fills in a box on the chart for each critical process identified for this CSF. In the *Exhibit*, for example, our team has listed "measure customer satisfaction," "monitor competition," "measure product quality," and seven other processes for its first CSF. Then the list must pass the sufficiency test. If all these activities are performed well, will the team achieve its first critical goal? If the team answers no, then it must identify what else is needed.

This is usually the stage at which teams begin to be really creative, looking beyond what is already being done and breaking new ground. There's a check, though, because each new process added for sufficiency must also have an owner within the management team. So it has to be important enough to feature on the matrix.

The team then repeats this process for each CSF in turn, being careful to apply the necessary-and-sufficient test before moving on to the next CSF. Then the number of CSFs that each process affects is totaled and placed in the count column on the right-hand side of the matrix.

By now the chart is a valuable document. The management team has agreed on its mission, on the subgoals, or CSFs, required to accomplish the mission, and finally, on the things that must be done to achieve those goals. Moreover, while each CSF is owned collectively by the entire team, each business process is owned by an individual member. Only one more step remains—identifying the most critical processes.

If companies had unlimited resources, each process could have equal attention for resources and management focus. But in practice, of course, managers' time and resources are always limited. So next pinpoint those activities that warrant the most attention.

Clearly, the most important processes are those that affect the most

CSFs. "Monitor competition," for example, affects six of the seven CSFs, so it is a strong candidate for scrutiny. But to get a meaningful ranking for management's attention, we also need to know how well each process is being performed.

In our PQM studies, we use a subjective ranking, which is entered in the quality column on the matrix. A = excellent performance, B = good performance, C = fair performance, D = bad performance, and E = informal or embryonic performance or indicates a process that's not performed at all. It may seem surprising, but we hear very few arguments about process quality. By this stage in the PQM process, the managers are really working as a team.

"Graphing makes priorities clear," the second part of the *Exhibit*, shows the best way we've found to help the team translate its rankings into an action plan. The quality of each process is plotted horizontally and the number of CSFs the process impacts is plotted vertically. Then the team divides the graph into zones to create groups of processes. We can see immediately that Zone 1 contains the most critical processes. All the processes are important, by definition. But the higher risk (or higher opportunity) processes are found in Zone 1. These activities need the team's closest attention if the company is to improve market share and profitability within two years.

Follow-through

That's the PQM process—one way to conduct what is, in truth, a never-ending journey to zero defects.

But as we said up front, PQM requires follow-through. Decide the nature of the improvement needed, and establish relevant process measurements. Then apply the needed resources for the appropriate improvements.

We cannot stress follow-through enough. The decisions reached by the management team must cascade throughout the organization. And always there are surprises. During one PQM process, it was discovered that not only was the process "define management responsibilities" one of the most critical at that time, it was also agreed that it was just not being done. This is the kind of function that everyone assumes is being done and someone else is doing it. Yet its poor performance (or nonexistence) can be a major inhibitor to success. The CEO immediately accepted ownership of that process and responsibility for its quality improvement.

We recommend revisiting the CSF list about once a year or whenever a significant change has taken place in a team's mission, its makeup, or the marketplace. In a year's time, the mission usually stays the same, but the critical success factors and the most critical processes usually don't. Some of the processes will have moved from Zone 1 to Zone 2; others will be newly critical.

If a company's CSFs remained constant while all of its business processes were being attended to, it would end up with zero-defect processes—and a justified reputation as a highly competitive company. But all kinds of things can alter a company's mission and goals: government, competitors, reorganization, new technology, new opportunities, the marketplace. And when you change the CSFs, you necessarily change the grid.

The next time a new matrix is produced, however, the business should be stronger and more flexible. If PQM has been applied, fewer existing processes will fall in quality category D or C. The average quality of business activities will be higher, and the biggest focus will be on new categories, the E processes, that the new CSFs demand. Eventually, you may even find that all your basic business activities are clustered in category A. Then the only changes a new CSF list will provoke are those responding to a changing environment. Such adaptability is the ultimate goal of PQM.

But does this mean the list of important processes is getting longer and longer and the matrix deeper and deeper? Not necessarily. Over time, what was once a most critical process will become sufficiently stable and well performed to allow its ownership to be delegated. And that's as it should be. ▽

*Seven steps to match your project's risk level
with your construction approach.*

You *Can* Manage Construction Risks

by John D. Macomber

Colossal County Hospital was coming apart at the seams. With dozens of newly hired doctors, nurses, and technicians, millions of dollars of equipment on the road, and patient appointments backed up for months, the new facility was impossible to use. For one thing, construction wasn't finished, and

 ## Construction is a service— not a product.

much of what was complete was faulty. Worse yet, the contractor had placed liens on the property for nonpayment, preventing occupancy. Costs had greatly outdistanced available financing. The hospital staff was frantic; the bank was apoplectic; the board of trustees was in despair.

How had it happened? The chairman of the board—head of the local branch of a financial services company—was baffled. He tried to trace the history of the project.

Two years earlier, the board members had voted to build an important new facility and renovate an adjoining older one. They hired the best available hospi-

tal architect. One group of trustees went on to focus its attention on a special bond issue to provide low-cost financing, while another group put together and executed a detailed marketing strategy to position the hospital as a world leader in several areas of care and research. Working closely with the doctors who would direct the various programs, the architect designed a state-of-the-art medical facility and a splendid building that would serve as a symbol for the hospital and as a landmark for the city.

On the architect's recommendation, a local contractor was retained to begin pricing the preliminary plans. As the drawings and budgeting progressed, the hospital was confident enough to apply for bank financing, and the bank, on the basis of the contractor's estimates and the proposed bond issue, agreed to make the loan.

John D. Macomber is vice president for strategic planning at George B.H. Macomber Company, Inc., a Boston-based construction company. Mr. Macomber also teaches a course entitled "Strategic Management of Engineering and Construction" in the Center for Construction Research and Education at the Massachusetts Institute of Technology.

Then the contractor presented his final budget. To the board's surprise, the estimate had grown by $3.5 million – and the detailed construction drawings still weren't complete. The contractor claimed the architect was upgrading the quality and scope of construction. The architect insisted he was only complying with the growing wish list of the trustees, doctors, and marketing experts hired by the board. But the bond issue was based on the original budget, and it wasn't big enough to accommodate the higher price. The hospital could not proceed. The trustees and the doctors held a meeting.

The doctors insisted they had added very little, and they refused to eliminate any of the medical features designed into the building. The trustees were convinced that the overall increase in scope was much smaller than the new price indicated. Everyone suspected the contractor of taking advantage of the hospital. The chairman decided it was time to act.

Wishful thinking about your project's budget can cause big trouble later on.

"In my industry – financial services," he reasoned, "all services are bid for. We give all aspirants a chance to say what they will charge. That's the way to get the lowest price."

A local manufacturer on the board agreed. "I had one of these 'trust me' contractors do my warehouse on a time-and-materials basis, and he soaked me good. He put his worst workers on the job, he didn't fight for purchase discounts, and he did everything he could to get costs up so his fee would go up. Let's not make the same mistake I made."

So the project was put out to bid with no modifications in scope and still without completed blueprints and specifications. Five companies submitted bids. The hospital's chief financial officer awarded the contract to a builder whose price was within the original budget. The original contractor was banished in disgrace, despite his protestations that his estimate was the right price for all the work the hospital would need.

Conflicts developed at once. The new builder had assumed that the space to be renovated would be vacated to work in, but the hospital couldn't do that. The builder threatened to stop work, so the board caved in and gave him an increase. The architect and the contractor fought constantly over interpretation of the drawings and specifications. The trustees, distracted by questions of finance and marketing, did not always make timely decisions. The con-

tractor cut every possible corner to hold down costs, and the architect overruled him again and again.

Just as the building was nearly finished, the board was shocked to receive a huge change-order request from the contractor alleging inaccurate specifications, changed conditions, and decision delays by the owner. The hospital refused to pay. The builder shut the job down and placed mechanic's liens on the property.

This was where the project now stood. The members of the board – successful local businesspeople, educators, and public servants – were angry and embarrassed; the architect was bitter; the original contractor was full of I-told-you-so's for anyone who'd listen. The chairman of the board was still baffled.

This story is exaggerated, of course, but parts of it are familiar to anyone who has been involved in a construction project. Building headaches are a fact of business life. Companies move. Businesses modernize old quarters. Growing organizations need more space. Companies incur some of their largest and longest term debts to finance these investments, while occupancy delays and construction quarrels can rank among the most debilitating problems a company can face. It is often impossible to predict exactly what a project will cost and how long it will take to complete, and it is always difficult to coordinate a dozen professionals – architects, engineers, contractors, bankers, lawyers, consultants, many with their own hidden agendas – and scores of subcontractors, suppliers, and workers.

All in all, the risks involved in a construction project are as great as any a company normally faces, and these risks are very different from the kind companies are used to. Yet many corporate officers and directors who consistently analyze and manage every other controllable risk fail to use all the tools available to control construction risk.

One reason CEOs and directors overlook or underestimate construction risk – and delegate it to subordinates to handle – is that construction is old technology. Buildings have been built before – what's so different about this one? The CFO is the watchdog for other expenses – why can't she watch these dollars too? The company has a department that does its purchasing – why can't it purchase a building? The facilities manager shares a vocabulary with the contractor – why not let him oversee the process? It seems foolish not to delegate a procedure that has been repeated a million times since the pyramids were finished.

But it is the exceptional CFO who can get beyond the first few summary numbers to understand what services a prospective contractor is really proposing;

it is the unusual purchasing agent who can oversee completion of a product containing tens of thousands of parts delivered over a period of up to several years; and facilities managers seldom have the expertise to defend their employers against contractors' claims. Finally, most companies do not go through the building process frequently. Construction skills are simply not part of a normal manager's repertoire.

Construction is a confusing process governed by complicated contracts and involving complex relationships in several tiers. The customer is really buying a service, not a product. At one relationship level, the contractor performs an essential service by directing and coordinating the work of dozens or hundreds of subcontractors, suppliers, craftspeople, and laborers. At the next level, someone – sometimes the contractor or the architect – must also coordinate the builder's services with those of the architects, engineers, and consultants. Finally, someone must take control of the entire process and coordinate the coordinators. At this level, the CEO and the board of directors will either manage the project and its risks or let the risks manage them. There is no substitute for responsibility at the top.

There are seven steps in the analysis and management of construction risk:

1. Understanding the types and phases of risk.
2. Assessing the risks of a particular construction project.
3. Matching risks with in-house capabilities and building a construction team.
4. Defining a building strategy.
5. Picking the right kind of contract.
6. Choosing the builder.
7. Monitoring construction.

Understanding the Types and Phases of Risk

There are three kinds of construction risk, and they surface in two phases. The first kind of risk is financial – the project exceeds its budget and endangers the financial health of the company. Budget overruns are not always a matter of poor construction supervision. They are often the result of bad planning, wishful pricing, or poor coordination.

The second kind of risk has to do with time – the building is finished behind schedule. Delays can have devastating financial consequences. What damage will your retail outlet suffer if its space is ready on January 4 instead of November 15? How will your organization function if the computer room is not ready because no one was ever assigned responsibility for ensuring uninterruptible power? What is the toll on your business if your CFO has to spend 40 days in a construction arbitration case?

The third type of risk is design-related – the completed building does not meet the organization's needs. For example, a health care organization with a fixed budget might elect to build a small addition with above-average finishwork and systems, only to discover on completion that it doesn't have enough space. (Perhaps it should have built a larger but plainer facility for the same money.) Or an office developer might pick an air-conditioning system that allows individual controls for each office but turns out to be too noisy. (A better match might have been to sacrifice individual controls to gain acoustic value or perhaps to spend more money to get both.)

All three kinds of risks can be addressed in both the *preconstruction phase* and the *construction-and-settlement phase.* The preconstruction phase is often the most grueling for the owner and often the most important. The organization must now make projections about marketing, budget, space, and schedule, and make actual decisions about design, zoning requirements, financing, traffic, and other environmental concerns. The risks in this phase are small in one sense because no one is actually building anything. But the risks are large in other ways. For one thing, consultants are expensive, and, since the construction loan is not yet in place, the company has to pay them out-of-pocket with unleveraged, highly speculative money. Also, a planning mistake or a piece of budgetary wishful thinking at this moment can cause big problems later on.

At this stage, Colossal County Hospital was already in trouble on three counts. First, the trustees were focusing on their individual specialties in marketing and finance, leaving the other preconstruction responsibilities to subordinates and doctors. Second, the architect dominated the preconstruction team and led it toward a design that would make more architectural and medical history than business sense. Third, the original contractor did not anticipate the growing wish lists, and, once he saw them, he was unable to convince the trustees that his new price was indeed reasonable – in fact, inescapable. The preconstruction team was poorly selected for the real needs of the project, and no one was in a position to monitor the team in detail and with authority.

There is a great deal of uncertainty and ambiguity in the preconstruction phase because the design-cost equation is constantly changing. A lot of hands-on specialists deal poorly with this lack of definition, and a poorly managed team can degenerate into chaos if the participants are allowed to hide behind their disciplines and stonewall or ignore each other.

The design-cost picture that emerges from this phase is the foundation on which great construction-period risk will rest, yet the work done now is the most manageable of the whole. Market and financial risks are external and uncontrollable. Preconstruction risk is internal to the team and can be controlled. The key to success in this phase, as elsewhere, is picking the right team–then providing coordination and central direction. The health care space and air-conditioning noise examples could both be best addressed in the preconstruction phase. Good use of the architect's and contractor's expertise at this juncture can save lots of problems later on.

In the construction-and-settlement phase, the risk factors move from planning to supervision. The design is mostly fixed; time risk no longer depends on creating a realistic schedule but on sticking to it; budgetary risk is no longer a matter of pricing but of cost control.

Yet appearances are deceptive. Depending on the contract, cost control is now mostly or entirely the contractor's responsibility. If your contract specified liquidated damages for late delivery, then schedule is the contractor's responsibility too, although most contracts allow several cost and schedule exceptions. What's more, a construction loan is now in place, so the bank reimburses the contractor directly for construction costs–usually on a monthly basis, always after carefully checking that the work has actually

Assessing construction risk is a matter of assessing complexity.

been done and the materials actually delivered, and almost always after holding back 5% to 10% of the total as a kind of performance guarantee until the entire project is complete and final settlement takes place. So where is the owner's risk?

Let's go back to Colossal County Hospital, a large institution brought to its knees at this very stage of the project. First of all, poor planning in the preconstruction phase came home to roost as the project drew to a close. For instance, the trustees had put the project out to bid on the basis of incomplete construction documents (blueprints and specifications), so the contractor had a right to adjust the price as the architect added new details. Second, while the bond issue set a limit on funds, the doctors and the architect fought to spend more, and the trustees never confronted the disparity. Third, the conditions of construction (the hospital's continued use of the space being renovated) and the trustees' repeated fail-

ure to make prompt decisions cost the contractor time, and such delays are legitimate grounds for a schedule extension. Finally, the mechanic's lien allows a contractor or subcontractor with a payment dispute to tie up a project in the courts and prevent its use or sale until the dispute is settled. And these are only a few of the problems that can crop up even after price, schedule, financing, payment mechanisms, and delivery date have supposedly been established once and for all.

As complex and as great as all these risks appear–particularly in the egregious case of Colossal County Hospital–it would be a waste of effort to try to eliminate every one of them, because that simply couldn't be done. The goal is to control and manage construction risk within reasonable limits.

Assessing the Risks of a Particular Construction Project

No two projects, no two sites, and no two construction teams are ever exactly the same. In order to pick the right team members, the right group of consultants, the right architect, the right contractor, and the right kind of contract, you need to understand the risks of your particular project. The crucial consideration is project complexity.

What are the company's needs for the project? Is there a rush for occupancy? Do you have time to develop complete blueprints and specifications before you put the project out to bid, or will you have to overlap this document preparation time with the start of construction? Are the mechanical systems routine, or will the contractor need to coordinate their design as well as installation? Is the quality of construction critical, as in a hospital, or do you need only a roof and walls? What about project financing? Some lenders will not make a commitment until they have seen the contracts and all of the completed drawings.

What about the site? There is a world of difference between building on a piece of well-drained farmland and building on a downtown site with an uncertain history and unknown conditions. Hazardous waste and the remains of old foundations are just two of the invisible surprises that are entirely the owner's responsibility in most contracts.

What about the structure? A new building will have many more components than an old one will, but a rehabilitation project will mean more unknowns and greater risks.

Evaluating the risk is the first step to controlling it. The chart, "Assessing Construction Risk," lists the

Assessing Construction Risk

Although many projects will have special risk factors of their own, this table lists the most important things to consider in assessing the risks of your project. The table is filled in for the situations of three hypothetical buildings. Colossal County Hospital is adding a new wing and renovating some older space on a crowded site in the middle of a city. Allperils Insurance is building a new, moderate-rise office structure in a suburban office park. Goodgoods Inc. is putting up a warehouse on former agricultural land near an interstate highway well away from populated areas.

■=High risk   ■=Moderate risk   ■=Low risk

Risk Elements	Colossal County Hospital	Allperils Insurance Company	Goodgoods Warehouse
Product			
Site			
Maneuvering room	No staging area	Office park; some constraints	Plenty of room
Neighbors	Residential and politicized	Cooperative	None
Soils	Sand and gravel	Peat and organics	Sand and gravel, some boulders
Traffic	Congested city streets	Coordinate with neighbors	Easy freeway access
Previous uses	Old foundations	Gas station site, buried tanks	None
Foundation			
Excavation	Retaining walls and underpinning	Open cut, some shoring	Open cut
Technology	Backhoe and steam shovel	Pressure-injected footings	Simple concrete mat
Structure			
Design	Beams and floors	Columns, beams, and floors	Bearing walls, joists, and deck
Materials	Cast-in-place concrete	Steel and concrete composite	Masonry, steel, concrete
Exterior			
Design	Complex: variety and details	Prefabricated metal panels	Stucco
Materials	Brick, stone, glass	Stainless steel	Stucco
Dimensional tolerance	Moderate	Low tolerance	High tolerance
Mechanical and electrical			
Heating-and-cooling plant	Cogeneration steam and electric	Gas-fired boiler and chiller	Electric heat, no A.C
Distribution	Hot-and-cold-water fan-coil units	Heat pumps	None
Communications	Hospital monitoring systems	Fiber-optic voice and data	None
Finishes			
Complexity	Moderate	Straightforward	Spartan
Materials	Moderate; paint and plaster	Marble and mahogany lobby	Paint, paneling, drywall
On-site craftsmanship	Durable more than memorable	Close tolerances	Serviceable
Sourcing	Local warehouse stock	Some special-order items	Local warehouse stock
End uses			
Flexibility intended	No; floor plans fixed	Partitions changeable	Highly flexible
Impact on business	Can't operate without it	Moving day can wait	Can't afford warehouse delay
Special situations	Renovation while space in use	None	None
Process			
Financing			
Preconstruction sources	Limited	In-house funds	In-house funds
Permanent financing	Reliable but inflexible	In-house funds	Traditional mortgage
Lender requirements	Strict; bonded contractor	Strict but self-administered	Lenient
Time			
Preconstruction time allowed	Years	Months	Weeks
Construction pace	Fast-track	Normal	Selected overtime work
Architecture			
Complexity of project	High	Suburban office standards	Low
Focus of designer	Make architectural history	Promote client image	Economy and ease of construction
Completeness of plans	Not enough for bid confidence	Complete	Essential items shown
Compensation to architect	High pay for quality designer	Moderate fee	Low fee for standard product
Owner's decision structure	Many committees and users	One small committee	One person
Need for "cooperative" input			
Rethinking of design option	Many preliminary designs	General program known	Few, if any
Relative number unknowns	Moderate; mostly new construction	Few	Very few
Budgeting expertise needed	Complex schedule and cost issues	Some (atrium, lobby pricing)	None beyond architect
Approvals			
Regulations and codes	Many agencies and rules	Standard life-safety codes	Basic building codes
Politics	Strong community support	Conformity standards	No issues

chief risk elements and shows how three hypothetical projects might have rated them.

Matching Risks with Capabilities and Building a Construction Team

Once you've estimated the risks of your project, the next step is to assess your organization's capacities. Building the construction team involves a series of classic make-or-buy decisions: What do we need? Can we provide it in-house? Should we buy it from outside? The chart, "Assessing In-House Capability," will help give you an idea of your organization's capacity to deal with the hundreds of construction headaches that will come up during the project.

Everyone knows that building a building requires a contractor and usually an architect, a couple of engineers, a lender, several consultants, and sometimes a lawyer. (Of all these professionals, there is only one you will have the freedom to choose as you please—the architect. See the box, "Choosing an Architect,"

> ## Subcontracts account for up to 80% of the cost of most commercial buildings.

for suggestions.) For the purposes of controlling risk, however, the principal players are your own board of directors, CEO, and senior staff, one or more of whom will actually oversee the entire project.

This person or persons—whom we might call the owner's representative (or even the developer)—will be at the center of a highly charged tangle of big egos, great stress, and high financial stakes. While the architect makes erudite speeches on aesthetics and design, the contractor may communicate mostly in profanities. While the banker speaks financial double-talk in hopes of reducing the lender's risk to zero, the heads of marketing and operations tear their hair out at the prospect of getting the wrong space at the wrong time. It takes a tough leader to coordinate everyone's efforts. If the CEO has the time and expertise, so much the better. If not, then he or she will have to delegate the responsibility to some unusual subordinate with the necessary breadth of knowledge and experience, or carefully assign parts of it to the architect or the contractor. But under no circumstances should coordination be delegated casually. Construction is one of the most argumentative industries on earth and the home of Murphy's Law—"If something can go wrong, it will."

Defining a Building Strategy

The charts have two important implications. First, they show how to identify and address the various individual elements of risk. Second, they define a strategy for the selection of a contractor and consultants. A concentration of high-risk components suggests you should look for the *performance* benefits of *cooperation* and try to find a contractor able to work as a team player. Predominantly low-risk components point instead to the *price* benefits of *competition*. Both kinds of contractors are readily available virtually everywhere.

The construction industry is highly fragmented and comparatively unsophisticated. Company strategies are often more intuitive than deliberate. Still, by choice or accident, construction companies lie somewhere on the spectrum between low-cost product providers at one end of the scale and highly differentiated service providers at the other. The challenge for clients is to identify the objective of each project and to pick the right fit.

Assessing In-House Capability

To make an adequate assessment of how much outside help you will need to get your building built, you need to look at your staff's talents. Basically, more in-house talent means less risk.

■=High risk   ■=Moderate risk   ■=Low risk

Capability	Colossal County Hospital	Allperils Insurance Company	Goodgoods Warehouse
Budgeting talent	One physical-plant veteran	Nobody	One former contractor in-house
Design talent	Nobody in-house	Nobody	Nobody
Team-building talent	No focus on this project	Moderate	One strong CEO
Monitoring talent	Finance experts, no construction experience	Finance experts, no construction experience	Nobody
Appetite for conflict	Board doesn't like conflicts	Well-developed	CEO happy to knock heads
Fund resources	No money for overruns	Can fund overruns in-house	Need to borrow more for overruns

Colossal County Hospital had a high-risk job and should have built a strong, cooperative team, including a contractor who would have worked closely with the board to solve problems. Instead, a board oriented too strongly toward competition made a decision solely on the basis of price and suffered the ill effects of an adversarial relationship with the builder. By contrast, the trustee who felt he'd been "soaked" on a time-and-materials contract for a warehouse did in fact waste money on cooperation. He should have had a competitive hard-money bid based on complete construction documents.

If your project is a simple, one-story building on a flat piece of vacant land, a low-cost provider is probably appropriate. The builder will not add much value beyond getting the material to the site and erecting it. If, on the other hand, your project is a complicated, fast-paced rehab, the noncraft services offered by a highly differentiated contractor may have great potential value. Your project may place special requirements on the contractor, like building one phase while the next is still being designed and priced; anticipating discovery of unknown conditions, like concealed rotting timbers; doing a workmanlike job from inadequate design documents; or working around existing occupants. Contractors who can do all this will charge more, but they will also act more like members of your team.

Another service the differentiated contractor can provide is to help you take advantage of the fragmentation of the building business by getting good competition among subcontractors. The commercial building industry is made up of thousands of subcontractors in several hundred specialized trades. These small companies tend to be entrepreneurial and fiercely independent, and their fractiousness can be a problem or an asset. Subcontracts and purchase orders can amount to 70% or 80% of the total cost of a commercial building project. Builders skilled at handling competition at the trade level may charge a higher fee for their own services and still produce the lowest total final cost.

Some contractors are also adept at forming value-adding partnerships with the subcontractors they use most often. Teams like these can gain efficiencies from shared design and production information as well as from a good understanding of each other's work styles. In this kind of cooperative setting, the game can have a sum higher than zero. Teamwork reduces friction, uncertainty, inefficiency, and duplication of effort.

Such teamwork is what Colossal County Hospital needed at every level. Of course, building teamwork requires energy and trust. As always, the question for management is whether the added value is worth the added cost. Colossal County didn't expend the energy or money to build the right team when it should have. Other owners may not need to.

Picking the Right Kind of Contract

The disparities among the levels of service outlined here have led to three main contract types. All three have been around for years, but many owners don't understand their relation to risk control. In most cases, a good evaluation of the kind and level of risk will point clearly to one of these three contracts.

The *lump-sum* contract is easy to understand. Each contractor bidding on the project estimates a total cost, adds a profit margin, and bids a fixed price for the job. The owner picks the lowest bid. If costs go up, the price to the owner remains the same. If costs go down—and the incentive to *make* them go down by cutting corners can be considerable—the extra margin goes to the contractor. This contract is truly a zero-sum game. Whatever the contractor gets is something you don't get.

With a lump-sum contract, the contractor takes all the visible risk, and the owner takes none. This seems like a good bet for high-risk projects, but just the opposite is true. First, should costs rise unexpectedly above the price that was bid and accepted, your contractor's dedication to the job may abruptly vanish. Second, with a lump-sum contract, the price may be fixed, but so is the scope of the work. Even a small change in the project can throw the whole contract out the window, and you cannot afford to renegotiate that contract once the work is under way. By avoiding risk, you also give up most of your decision-making power. In other words, you pay your money and you take your chances—which is no way to build a hospital or any other highly differentiated structure. Still, the lump-sum contract is the right contract for simple jobs where price is more important than collaboration.

Most people are familiar with *time-and-materials* contracts—based on the cost of work plus a fee. Lawyers bill this way, and so do auto mechanics. The builder gets reimbursed for the actual costs of the work, whatever they are, plus a percentage fee or markup. So, in other words, the owner takes all the risk and the contractor none. The customer can be fairly certain that work will be properly done, because there is no incentive to cut corners. Of course, the more the contractor spends, the more the contractor makes—and we know from experience that auto mechanics and lawyers have no particular incentive to hurry.

Choosing an Architect

Even if you've never managed a building project, you can still help your company find a suitable architect. Here are some tips for making the right choice:

1. *Name a design committee.* As soon as you've established the need for a building project, set up a committee. Members will likely include the CEO, the CFO, probable users, and maintenance staff. Decide how the architect will be chosen—by consensus, majority vote, or executive decision.

2. *Outline the project.* The committee must start by agreeing on a project program. Clarify what you need and want in a building. Think about goals, schedule, budget, and locations. Decide what matters most—speed, cost, design—and make a preliminary assessment of risk. For all its technical expertise, the design firm is only a consultant. There is no substitute for the owner's overall direction.

3. *Decide on a selection process.* Expensive design competitions are appropriate for museums and multinational headquarters buildings. The usual method—much preferred by architects—is prequalification and interview.

4. *Make a preliminary list of architects.* Get a list of local design firms. Ask friends, business associates, and your facilities managers for names. Prestige is less important than matching the architect with the scope of the challenges. Send a "request for qualifications" (RFQ) to likely firms. This can simply be a letter describing the project and asking interested design firms to submit their credentials.

5. *Shorten the list.* When the RFQ responses have come in and you've reduced the list to no more than about a dozen candidates, follow up with an RFP (request for proposals) to help you decide which firms to interview. Of course, the amount of detail you can expect from design firms in response to an RFP will depend on how much information you give them and how many contenders have a shot at the job. In assessing proposals, consider the following (the first two are the most important):

☐ Proposed project team. Will the firm's principals work on your project day-to-day? If not, who will?

☐ Budget-and-schedule track record. Staying within the financial and time constraints is critical.

☐ Size of firm and length of practice. Big firms have depth, but a small firm just might give you more personalized service.

☐ Recent project history. Look for similar clients and building types, but remember that no two projects are ever exactly the same.

☐ Location. Local firms have a decided advantage in dealing with local authorities and regulations. Distant firms can reduce their disadvantage by working with a local architect.

☐ Special expertise. Rehabs are different from new construction; urban and suburban areas are different; historic preservation is a special skill.

☐ Knowledge of codes. Coordination of electrical and mechanical systems with layout and furnishings is the architect's responsibility before it becomes the contractor's.

☐ Supervisory experience. If the design firm will be supervising construction, make sure it knows how.

☐ Fee proposal. Architects can propose a fee only if you've defined project goals and scope enough to give them a clear sense of the job.

6. *Interview the short list.* The interviews will be interesting and entertaining—design firms are good at this—but don't be seduced by slides, models, and a lot of talk about the design process. Ask about the firm's approach to cost estimating and cost control; experience in getting local government approvals and handling public hearings; procedures for solving design problems; relations with the special technical consultants the project will require. Otherwise, the interview should be an elaboration of the RFP response. Make a particular point of discussing the firm's experience with construction bidding and the different kinds of contracts. Finally, make sure that the key figures on the project team are at the interview, and be sure you're comfortable with the personalities you'll be working with. From time to time, your architect will probably have to read your mind in order to turn your wishes into blueprints. Ask yourself if this is the firm that can translate your personal vision into concrete detail.

7. *Check references.* Interviewing will give you specific questions to ask of references. Ask particularly about cost control, schedule compliance, and problem solving. Find out which individuals worked on the project, and speak to them. Your principal question is whether the previous client would use the same architect again, and why or why not. Visit finished buildings and talk to their users.

8. *Get off to a good start.* Once you understand your own goals, choosing the right architect is a matter of combining thoughtful questions with common sense. When your decision is made, notify the unsuccessful candidates and give each an explanation of your choice. Then the real challenge begins—working with the chosen architect to satisfy your company's needs.

—KATHY A. SPIEGELMAN

Kathy A. Spiegelman is director of physical planning at Harvard University. She guides and oversees the architect selection process for all Harvard construction projects.

Despite the obvious disadvantages in terms of risk, there are three fairly common situations—and one fairly uncommon one—where time-and-materials is nevertheless the right contract for the owner. The first is when quality matters more than money. The second is when time is very limited and the contractor will have to work extensive overtime. The third is when construction documents are incomplete or missing, which leaves the contractor nothing on which to base a bid. The fourth situation comes up when owners have so much construction expertise and so much time to devote to supervision that they can get exactly what they want and still hold down costs by directing the location and quality of every brick and nail.

For most situations, one of these two contracts will fit the bill. But for many large construction users, a hybrid form called *guaranteed-maximum-price* is more appropriate. It is often the best contract for performing the work identified as high-risk in the two charts.

Like time-and-materials, guaranteed-maximum-price is also based on the cost of work plus a fee, but risk is shared. Up to the predetermined maximum price, the contractor passes along all costs to the owner, but once that price is reached, all risk belongs to the builder.

As in a time-and-materials contract, the owner benefits when direct costs are less than expected. But when costs go up too far, contractors absorb the overrun, as they would in a lump-sum contract. Generally, this arrangement keeps the best features of both other contract types and allows the owner to have his cake and eat it too. Most often, the guaranteed maximum price will be set higher than the lump-sum price for the same project because the contractor's profit is capped.

The goal in this case is to make contractors team players without giving them carte blanche. The construction company's profit does not depend on cost cutting but rather on good performance of this service for the owner. What the customer gets is a limit on exposure and a cooperative relationship instead of an adversarial one.

The exhibit, "Cost vs. Price with the Three Contract Types," shows price in relation to actual construction cost in lump-sum, time-and-materials, and guaranteed-maximum-price contracts.

These three contract types all assume the traditional owner-architect-contractor configuration. There are three less common ways to assign these roles. With a *turnkey* contract, the owner buys site, design, and finished building as a package. The supplier secures the construction financing and plays the role of owner and contractor (and sometimes architect) during construction. Turnkey contracts are suited to situations where the needs of the user are easily described.

A *design-build* contract is very like a turnkey contract in that the architect and contractor work under one contract, giving one source of responsibility. This fosters cooperation at the cost of eliminating traditional checks and balances. But in design-build, as opposed to turnkey, the owner is responsible for financing.

Construction management, in its simplest form, is merely a consulting service. Construction managers often supplement the owner's in-house construction team by giving advice and providing supervision for a fee. They take no fiduciary responsibility, and they do not guarantee price, results, or schedule. (Be aware that architects, engineers, contractors, and consultants all use the phrase "construction management" a little differently. Before you contract for construction management, make sure you know exactly what you're getting.)

Choosing the Builder

It sounds elementary at this point to say that the way a company chooses a builder should match its project-risk level and contract type. But the old practice of bidding out contracts is so well established that organizations resort to it even when it makes no sense. Each kind of project and contract should have its own selection criteria.

Lump-sum. The builder for a lump-sum contract can be chosen almost entirely by means of an open bid based on construction documents—blueprints and specifications—that clearly define the scope of the work. (Never put partial documents out to bid. In fact, if you must choose a contractor before the documents are done, lump-sum may be the wrong type of contract.) Beyond requiring bidders to satisfy some minimum level of experience, reputation, and financial strength, price is really all you care about.

One warning: Resist the temptation to take advantage of a very low bid. It may be a mistake based on misinterpreted construction documents, and the ensuing fight won't be worth it.

Time-and-materials. For a so-called cost-plus or time-and-materials contract, reputation, ability, and trust are paramount. Check references, look for the right chemistry between all parties, make sure you are comfortable with the builder. Whatever you do, don't try to make a selection on the basis of some kind of estimated bid. If the contract has no cap, the bid means nothing. It can only tempt you to choose

Cost vs. Price with the Three Contract Types *(in thousands of dollars)*

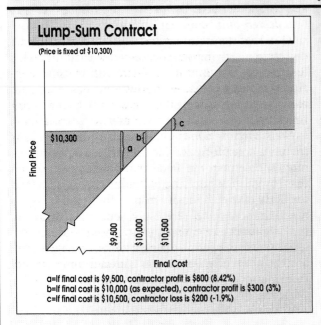

Lump-Sum Contract

(Price is fixed at $10,300)

a=If final cost is $9,500, contractor profit is $800 (8.42%)
b=If final cost is $10,000 (as expected), contractor profit is $300 (3%)
c=If final cost is $10,500, contractor loss is $200 (-1.9%)

Assume that the contractor believes your project will wind up costing just about $10 million to build. These three graphs show the price to you and the profit or loss to the contractor for three different kinds of contracts at three different actual final cost levels. At point *a* in each diagram, the contractor has shaved $500,000 from the anticipated cost. At *b*, costs have run as expected. At *c*, there has been a cost overrun of $500,000. Basically, with a *lump-sum*, the contractor gets all the savings and takes all the risk. With *time-and-materials*, the owner gets the savings and takes the risk. And with *guaranteed-maximum-price*, the owner gets the savings, the builder takes the risk.

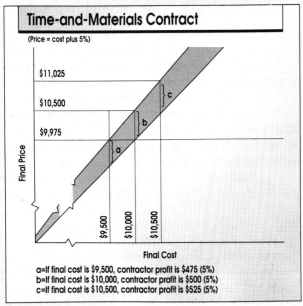

Time-and-Materials Contract

(Price = cost plus 5%)

a=If final cost is $9,500, contractor profit is $475 (5%)
b=If final cost is $10,000, contractor profit is $500 (5%)
c=If final cost is $10,500, contractor profit is $525 (5%)

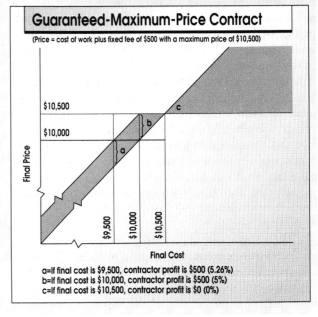

Guaranteed-Maximum-Price Contract

(Price = cost of work plus fixed fee of $500 with a maximum price of $10,500)

a=If final cost is $9,500, contractor profit is $500 (5.26%)
b=If final cost is $10,000, contractor profit is $500 (5%)
c=If final cost is $10,500, contractor profit is $0 (0%)

the lowest of several meaningless numbers, and that is a good way to pick the least competent candidate.

Guaranteed-maximum-price. The process here is much like the one above. Your guide should be the contractor's experience, references, and integrity, and the chemistry between you. You are planning to pay a fee to a company for its competence in managing construction, meeting schedules, maintaining quality, providing construction services, and treating its clients honestly and fairly. Establishing that competence should be your only criterion.

Any company in the running for this type of contract will be able to give you the names of previous customers who can tell you just how well it performed in the past. Ask about the accuracy of the cost estimates and the extent of the savings returned to the owner (or the size of the overrun absorbed by the contractor). Ask how many serious fights there were and whether they were settled satisfactorily. Find out if the space was delivered on time. Ask for references from former subcontractors as well, and find out what they thought of the company they worked for.

You are buying a value-added service. Make sure you will get what you're paying for.

Monitoring Construction

Everybody likes to watch excavating equipment and play sidewalk superintendent when the big steel flies. Monitoring the team and the contract is much less fun—and much more important. Once again, the scope and method of supervision depends on the kind of contract.

On a lump-sum contract, the developer or the owner's representative must monitor both materials and workmanship to make sure the contractor does not pad his or her own profit by delivering less than what was contracted for. This level of attention calls for a construction supervisor who understands specifications, details, workmanship, and materials gradation and handling.

On a time-and-materials contract, the construction supervisor's job is to see that the contractor doesn't waste the owner's money. The builder will not likely cut corners, but cost control probably won't be a top priority either. This kind of contract needs a monitor who understands labor productivity, effective use of raw materials, and cost accounting.

In theory, the structure of a guaranteed-maximum-price contract reduces the degree of supervision the owner will need. The contractor assumes the risk of a cost overrun and earns a predetermined fee to make sure that the work and the materials are right. Still, a prudent owner will keep an eye on workmanship and accounting. The skills of an experienced construction supervisor must still be available, but the need is less urgent.

Clearly, the person who acts as construction supervisor needs experience and expertise. Few CEOs—and few members of the board—would qualify. If the project coordinator is not a construction expert, it may sometimes be worthwhile to hire a construction consultant. Often the architect is used for construction supervision, and sometimes this works

very well. But architects are trained to design, and their capacity and willingness to check on workmanship, monitor materials, and oversee accounting is at best uneven.

Then, too, as projects grow more complex, the architect has a progressively greater need to work with, not against, the contractor. There will always be issues of interpretation, aesthetics, even cost, for them to consider together. And in a project with many unknown risks—a building with marine foundations, say, or the renovation of a historic structure—the contractor's experience and judgment are crucial assets for the architect. An owner's insistence on police duty can impair an architect's ability to work with the builder.

Colossal County Hospital survived its ordeal—the city intervened with an emergency loan and a supplemental bond issue—and learned from the experience. For its next addition, the board built a team from the beginning and stayed abreast of the process. The new chairman of the board, head of a local management consulting firm, took on the role of in-house developer. She led the team through a preconstruction analysis of complexity and risk that then drove the choice of contract, builder, financing, and schedule. The chosen contractor had a reputation for accurate pricing and cooperative problem solving. The project came in on time and even slightly under budget.

The manufacturing trustee learned his lesson too. For his new distribution center, he hired an architect who could provide him with dependable, detailed drawings; he put the project out to bid only when all of the specifications and blueprints were complete; and he chose the low bidder from a field of 12 prequalified builders. The space cost him 50% less than with the earlier time-and-materials contract.

Construction is a major obligation for many growing companies. The initial estimates of cost, time, and trouble are bound to change dramatically as work progresses. The construction team itself may be volatile and problematic. But the directors and top management of your company can identify, analyze, and rationally control these risks.

Reprint 89210

Knowing when to pull the plug

*Barry M. Staw and
Jerry Ross*

Last year you authorized the expenditure of $500,000 for what you thought was a promising new project for the company. So far, the results have been disappointing. The people running the project say that with an additional $300,000 they can turn things around. Without extra funding, they cry, there is little hope. Do you spend the extra money and risk further losses, or do you cut off the project and accept the half-million-dollar write-off?

Managers face such quandaries daily. They range from developing and placing employees to choosing plant sites and making important strategic moves. Additional investment could either remedy the situation or lead to greater loss. In many situations, a decision to persevere only escalates the risks, and good management consists of knowing when to pull the plug.

> *Perseverance is important.
> It can also be self-defeating.*

These escalation situations are trouble. Most of us can think of times when we should have bailed out of a course of action. The Lockheed L 1011 fiasco and the Washington Public Supply System debacle (commonly referred to as WHOOPS) are spectacular examples of organizational failure to do so. Decisions to persist with these crippled ventures caused enormous losses.

Of course, all managers will make some mistakes and stick with some decisions longer than they ought to. Recent research has shown, however, that the tendency to pursue a failing course of action is not a random thing. Indeed, at times some managers, and even entire organizations, seem almost programmed to follow a dying cause.[1]

What leads executives to act so foolishly? Are they people who should never have been selected for responsible positions? Are these organizations simply inept? Or are they generally competent managers and companies that find themselves drawn into decisional quicksand, with many forces driving them deeper? Though we think this last description is probably the right one, we don't think the tendency is uncheckable. Managers and organizations that often fall into escalation traps can take steps to avoid them.

Why projects go out of control

As a start to understanding why people get locked into losing courses of action, let's look first at what a purely rational decision-making approach would be. Consider, for example, the decision to pursue or scuttle an R&D or a marketing project. On the basis of future prospects, you'd have made the initial decision to pursue the project, and enough time would have passed to see how things were going. Ideally, you'd then reassess the situation and decide on future action. If you were following a fully rational approach, whatever losses might have occurred before this decision point would be irrelevant for your reassessment. With a cold, clear eye, you'd view the prospects for the future as well as your available options. Would the company be better off if it got out, continued with the project, or decided to invest more resources in it? You'd treat any previous expenses or losses as sunk costs, things that had happened in the past, not to be considered when you viewed the future.

In theory, pure rationality is great, but how many managers and organizations actually follow

Mr. Staw is the Mitchell Professor of Leadership and Communication at the Schools of Business Administration at the University of California in Berkeley. He is also chairman of its Organizational Behavior and Industrial Relations Group.

Mr. Ross is associate professor of organizational behavior at the Graduate School of Industrial Administration at Carnegie-Mellon University.

it? Not many. Instead, several factors encourage decision makers to become locked into losing courses of action.

The project itself

The first set of factors have to do with the project itself. "Is the project not doing well because we omitted an important factor from our calculations, or are we simply experiencing the downside of problems that we knew could occur?" "Are the problems temporary [bad weather or a soon-to-be-settled supplier strike] or more permanent [a steep downturn in demand]?" Expected or short-term problems are likely to encourage you to continue a project. You may even view them as necessary costs or investments for achieving large, long-term gains. If you expect problems to arise, when they do, they may convince you that things are going as planned.

A project's salvage value and closing costs can also impede withdrawal. An executive could simply terminate an ineffective advertising campaign in midstream, but stopping work on a half-completed facility is another story. A project that has very little salvage value and high closing costs – payments to terminated employees, penalties for breached contracts, and losses from the closing of facilities – will be much more difficult to abandon than a project in which expenditures are recoverable and exit is easy. It's understandable why so many financially questionable construction projects are pursued beyond what seems to be a rational point of withdrawal.[2]

Consider the Deep Tunnel project in Chicago, a plan to make a major addition to the city's sewer system that will eventually improve its capacity to handle major storms. Although the project has absorbed millions of dollars, it won't deliver any benefits until the entire new system is completed. Unfortunately, as each year passes, the expected date of completion recedes into the future while the bill for work to be finished grows exponentially. Of course, no one would have advocated the project if the true costs had been known at the outset. Yet, once begun, few have argued to kill the project.

The problem is that the project was structured in ways that ensured commitment. First, the project managers viewed each setback as a temporary situation that was correctable over time with more money. Second, they perceived all moneys spent as investments toward a large payoff they'd reap when the project was complete. Third, expenditures were irretrievable: the laid pipe in the ground has no value unless the entire project is completed, and it would probably cost more to take the pipe out of the ground than it's worth. Thus, like many other large construction

and R&D projects, investors in the Deep Tunnel have been trapped in the course of action. Even though what they receive in the end may not measure up to the cost of attaining it, they have to hang on until the end if they hope to recoup any of their investment.

Managers' motivations

Most of the factors concerning projects that discourage hanging on are evident to managers. They may not fully factor closing costs and salvage value into their initial decisions to pursue certain courses of action (since new ventures are supposed to succeed rather than fail), but when deciding whether to continue a project or not, executives are usually aware of these factors. Less obvious to managers, however, are the psychological factors that influence the way information about courses of action are gathered, interpreted, and acted on.

We are all familiar with the idea that people tend to repeat behavior if they are rewarded and to stop it if they are punished. According to the theory of reinforcement, managers will withdraw from a course of action in the face of bad news. This interpretation, however, ignores people's history of rewards. Managers have often been rewarded for ignoring short-run disaster, for sticking it out through tough times. Successful executives – people whose decisions have turned out to be winners even when the outlook had appeared grim – are particularly susceptible. It's tough for managers with good track records to recognize that a certain course isn't a satisfactory risk, that things aren't once again going to turn their way.

Reinforcement theory also tells us that when people receive rewards intermittently (as from slot machines), they can become quite persistent. If a decline in rewards has been slow and irregular, a person can go on and on even after the rewards have disappeared. Unfortunately, many business situations that escalate to disaster involve precisely this type of reinforcement pattern. Sales may fall slowly in fits and starts, all the while offering enough hope that things will eventually return to normal. The hope makes it difficult to see that the market may have changed in fundamental ways. Revenues that slowly sour or costs that creep upward are just the kind of pattern that can cause managers to hang on beyond an economically rational point.

Research has also shown other reasons that executives fail to recognize when a project is beyond hope. People have an almost uncanny ability to see only what accords with their beliefs. Much like sports fans who concentrate on their own team's great plays and the other team's fouls, managers tend to see only what confirms their preferences. For example, an executive who is convinced that a project will be profitable will probably slant estimates of sales and costs to support the view. If the facts challenge this opinion, the manager may work hard to find reasons to discredit the source of information or the quality of the data. And if the data are ambiguous, the manager may seize on just those facts that support the opinion. Thus information biasing can be a major roadblock to sensible withdrawal from losing courses of action.

In addition to the effects of rewards and biased information, a third psychological mechanism may be at work. Sometimes even when managers recognize that they have suffered losses, they may choose to invest further resources in a project rather than accept failure. What may be fostering escalation in these cases is a need for self-justification. Managers may interpret bad news about a project as a personal failure. And, like most of us who are protective of our self-esteem, managers may hang on or even invest further resources to "prove" the project a success.

A number of experiments have verified this effect of self-justification. Those who are responsible for previous losses, for example, have generally been found to view projects more positively and to be more likely to commit additional resources to them than are people who have taken over projects in midstream. Managers who are not responsible for previous losses are less likely to "throw good money after bad" since they have less reason to justify previous mistakes.[3]

Reinforcement, information biasing, and self-justification—three psychological factors that we're all subject to—can keep us committed to projects or actions we have started. Most managerial decisions, however, involve some additional factors that come into play when other people are around to observe our actions. These are social determinants.

Social pressures

Managers may persist in a project not only because they don't want to admit error to themselves but also because they don't wish to expose their mistakes to others. No one wants to appear incompetent. Though persistence may be irrational from the organization's point of view, from the point of view of the beleaguered manager seeking to justify past behavior, it can be quite understandable. When a person's fate is tied to demands for performance and when accepting failure means loss of power or loss of a job, hanging on in the face of losses makes sense. Research has shown, for example, that job insecurity and lack of managerial support only heighten the need for external justification.[4] Thus when a manager becomes closely identified with a project ("that's Jim's baby"), he can be

essentially forced to defend the venture despite mounting losses and doubts about its feasibility.

Beyond the personal risks of accepting losses, our ideas of how a leader should act can also foster foolish persistence. Culturally, we associate persistence—"staying the course," "sticking to your guns," and "weathering the storm"—with strong leadership. Persistence that happens to turn out successfully is especially rewarded. For example, when we think about the people who have become heroes in business and politics (Iacocca and Churchill, for examples), we see leaders who have faced difficult and apparently failing situations but who have hung tough until they were successful. If people see persistence as a sign of leadership and withdrawal as a sign of weakness, why would they expect managers to back off from losing courses of action? Recent research demonstrates that even though it may not add to the welfare of the organization, persistence does make a manager look like a leader.[5]

In short, the need to justify one's actions to others and to appear strong as a leader can combine with the three psychological factors to push managers into staying with a decision too long. This combination of forces does not, however, account for all debacles in which organizations suffer enormous losses through excessive commitment. In many of these cases structural factors also play a role.

Organizational pushes & pulls

Probably the simplest element impeding withdrawal from losing projects is administrative inertia. Just as individuals do not always act on their beliefs, organizations do not always base their practices on their preferences. All the rules, procedures, and routines of an organization as well as the sheer trouble it takes for managers to give up day-to-day activities in favor of a serious operational disruption can cause administrative inertia. Dropping a line of business may mean changing corporate layoff policies, and moving people to other projects may violate seniority and hiring procedures. Sometimes it's just easier not to rock the boat.

Beyond such simple inertia, the politics of a situation can prevent a bailout. British Columbia's decision to stage the world's fair Expo '86 is one of the most recent public examples of the power of political forces to sustain a costly course of action. Expo '86 was supposed to operate close to the financial break-even point. But as plans for the fair got under way, the expected losses burgeoned. At first, the planners tried to minimize the financial hazards by providing heartening but biased estimates of revenues and costs. When they finally accepted the more dire financial projections, however, and even the director recommended cancellation, the planners still went ahead with the fair. Politically it was too late: the fortunes of too many businesses in the province were tied to Expo, it was popular with the voters, and the future of the premier and his political party were aligned with it. The province created a lottery to cope with the expected $300 million deficit, and the fair opened as scheduled.

Though the Expo example comes from the public sector, political force may also sustain costly business projects. As a venture withers, not only those directly involved with it may work to maintain it, but other interdependent or politically aligned units may support it as well. If the project's advocates sit on governing bodies or budget committees, efforts to stop it will meet further resistance. If a review finally does occur, the estimates of the costs and benefits of continuing the venture will very likely be biased.

On occasion, support for a project can go even deeper than administrative inertia and politics. When a project such as a long-standing line of business is closely identified with a company, to consider its discontinuation is to consider killing the very purpose of the company. (Imagine Hershey without chocolate bars or Kimberly-Clark without Kleenex.) A project or a division can become institutionalized in an organization.

Consider the plight of Lockheed with its L 1011 Tri-Star Jet program. Although every outside analysis of the program found the venture unlikely to earn a profit, Lockheed persisted with it for more than a decade and accumulated enormous losses. The problem was not ending the project per se but what it symbolized. The L 1011 was Lockheed's major entry in the commercial aviation market (in which it had been a pioneer), and Lockheed shrank from being identified as simply a defense contractor.

Pan American World Airways has recently gone through a similar institutional process. More than most airlines, Pan Am suffered huge losses after deregulation of the industry; it was even in danger of not meeting its debt obligations. Although the prospects for large profits in the airline industry were dim, Pan Am chose to sell off most of its other more profitable assets—first the Pan Am building in New York and then the Intercontinental Hotels Corporation—so as to remain in its core business. Finally, as losses continued, Pan Am sold its valuable Pacific routes to United Air Lines. Following these divestitures, the company was left with only U.S. and international routes in corridors where competition is heavy. Apparently, management didn't seriously consider the possibility of selling or closing the airline and keeping most of the other profitable subsidiaries. Pan Am is, after all, in the airline and not the real estate or hotel business.

Not all the forces we've described are relevant to every case, and not all are of equal influence in the situations where they operate. In many instances, commitment to a course of action builds slowly. Psychological and social forces come into play first, and only later does the structure make its impact. And, in a few cases, because the rational point of withdrawal has long passed, even the economic aspects of a project can cry out for continuation.

Still, some executives do manage to get themselves and entire organizations out of escalating situations. There *are* solutions.

Steps executives can take themselves

Executives can do many things to prevent becoming overcommitted to a course of action. Some of these solutions they can take care of on their own. Others involve getting the organization to do things differently. Let's look first at the remedies that executives themselves can apply.

Recognize overcommitment

The most important thing for managers to realize is that they may be biased toward escalation. For all the reasons we have mentioned, executives may delude themselves into thinking that a project will pull through—that success is around the corner. Recognizing overcommitment is, however, easier to preach than to practice. It usually takes enthusiasm, effort, and even passion to get projects off the ground and running in bureaucratic organizations. The organization depends on these responses for vitality. Consequently, the line between an optimistic, can-do attitude and overcommitment is very thin and often difficult to distinguish.

See escalation for what it is

How, then, can managers know whether they have crossed the threshold between the determination to get things done and overcommitment? Although the distinction is often subtle, they can clarify matters by asking themselves the following questions:

1   Do I have trouble defining what would constitute failure for this project or decision? Is my definition of failure ambiguous, or does it shift as the project evolves?

2   Would failure on this project radically change the way I think of myself as a manager or as a person? Have I bet the ranch on this venture for my career or for my own satisfaction?

3   Do I have trouble hearing other people's concerns about the project, and do I sometimes evaluate others' competence on the basis of their support for the project?

4   Do I generally evaluate how various events and actions will affect the project before I think about how they'll affect other areas of the organization or the company as a whole?

5   Do I sometimes feel that if this project ends, there will be no tomorrow?

If a manager has answered yes to one or more of these questions, the person is probably overcommitted to a project.

Back off

Just knowing that one is under the sway of escalation can help. But knowing is not enough. It is also necessary to take some steps to avoid overcommitment. One way is to schedule regular times to step back and look at a project from an outsider's perspective. A good question to ask oneself at these times is, "If I took over this job for the first time today and found this project going on, would I support it or get rid of it?" Managers could take their cues from bankers. When they take over others' portfolios, bankers usually try to clean up any troubled loans since they want to maximize the future returns associated with their own loan activity. Managers can also encourage their subordinates to reevaluate decisions. Most critical here is establishing a climate in which, regardless of whether the data are supportive or critical of the ongoing project, people convey accurate information. Just stating a "nothing but the truth" policy, however, is usually not enough to change the pattern of information reporting. The messenger with extremely critical but important information needs an explicit reward.

> *Some managers seem programmed to follow dying causes.*

One forum for getting objective and candid feedback is a variant of the currently popular quality circle. Managers could regularly convene key staff members for "decision circles," in which fellow employees would offer honest evaluations of the hurdles a project faces and its prospects. Managers from other departments or sections might also attend or even chair such sessions to ensure an objective look at the problems. Managers might also hold regular "exchanges of perspective" in which colleagues could help each other see the truth about their operations.

Change the organization

Though it is possible to come up with an array of decision aids to help managers gain an objective perspective about the projects they run, one could argue that the problem of escalation is larger than any one person, that it's organizational in scope. Unfortunately, such a pessimistic view is at least partially correct. Much of what causes escalation is in the nature of organizations, not people.

If organizational action is called for, what can the system do to minimize escalation?

Turn over administrators

One way to reduce the commitment to a losing course of action is to replace those associated with the original policy or project. If overcommitment stems from psychological and social forces facing the originators of the action, then their removal eliminates some of the sources of commitment.

Turning over project managers can of course be both disruptive and costly. Moreover, because people who were once associated with the discontinued venture may still be committed to it, management may find it difficult to draw the appropriate line for making a purge. Nonetheless, to make a clean break with the past, many organizations do make occasional personnel sweeps, sometimes more for their symbolic value than because of any real differences in decision making.

Still, we don't recommend turnover as the way to make changes. Like treating the disease by killing the patient, taking committed decision makers off a project may produce nothing but a demoralized staff and disaffected managers hesitant to try again.

Separate decision makers

One technique for reducing commitment that is far less drastic than turnover is to separate initial from subsequent decisions concerning a course of action. In some banks, for example, a "workout group" handles problem loans rather than the people who originally funded and serviced the loans. The idea is not only that specialists should be involved in recouping bank funds but also that these officers are able to handle the loans in a more objective way than those who made the first decisions about the accounts.[6] Industrial companies could also make use of such procedures. They could separate funding from new-product-development decisions and hiring from promotion decisions. They could keep deliberations on whether to discontinue lines of business apart from day-to-day management decisions.

Reduce the risk of failure

Another way to reduce commitment is to lessen the risk of failure. Because project failure can spell the end to an otherwise promising career, an administrator may be forced to defend a losing course of action. In a no-win dilemma, the trapped manager may think, "Things look bleak now, but there's no point in my suggesting that the company withdraw. If the project doesn't succeed, I have no future here anyway."

In some companies, management has reduced the costs of failure by providing rationalizations for losing courses of action and excuses for their managers. People are told that the losses are beyond anyone's control or that the fault lies with more general economic conditions, government regulation, or foreign competition. Although this route takes managers off the hook, it doesn't help them see a losing course for what it is or how they may avoid making the mistakes again.

Most companies do not want to take the pressure off their managers to perform as winners. Yet because a strong fear of failure can cause overcommitment, management is better off setting only a moderate cost for failure, something to avoid but not to fear intensely. A large computer company, for example, puts managers who have made big mistakes in a "penalty box." It makes them ineligible for major assignments for up to a year. After the penalty period, the managers are restored to full status in the organization and are again eligible to run major projects. Organizations trying to cope with escalation situations may find such a compromise between support for failure and demand for competence helpful.

Improve the information system

Several laboratory experiments have shown that people will withdraw from escalating situations when they see the high costs of persisting.[7] The presentation of such negative data is more difficult in organizations, however. Because no one wants to be the conveyer of bad news, information is filtered as it goes up the hierarchy. Furthermore, because those intimately involved with a project are not likely to distribute unflattering and less-than-optimistic forecasts, information is also biased at the source.

What, then, can organizations do to improve their information reporting? The most common solution is to increase their use of outside experts and consultants. The problem with consultants, however, is that they are no more likely to hear the truth than anyone else in the organization, and they also may not find it easy to tell management what it doesn't want to hear.

A better solution is to try to improve the honesty of reporting throughout the organization. By rewarding process as highly as product, managers can encourage candid reporting. The purpose of rewarding managers for the way a process is carried out is to make them attend as much to the quality of analysis and decision making as to the final results. Instead of acting as champions who inflate the prospects of their own projects and minimize their risks, managers offered process rewards are motivated to recognize problems and deal with them.

At the outset of projects, companies should encourage the creation of fail-safe options, ways to segment projects into small, achievable parts, and analyses of the costs of withdrawal. Later in the life of projects, companies should reward honest recognition of problems and clear examination of the alternatives, including withdrawal.

This kind of reward system is quite different from the usual practice of giving people recognition for success on their projects and punishing them for failure on their undertakings. Yet it is a system that should reduce many of the forces for escalation.

Boosting experimentation

As we noted earlier in our discussion, an entire organization can be so caught up in supporting a project—especially an institutionalized one—that it ignores the cost of persistence.

Rather than trying to discredit an institutionalized project on economic grounds, a good strategy for withdrawal from it is to reduce its links with the central purposes of the organization. A useful tactic is to label the project peripheral or experimental so that managers can treat it on its own merits rather than as a symbol of the organization's central goal or mission.

Ideally, managers should consider all ventures imperfect and subject to question in an "experimenting organization."[8] Every program should be subject to regular reconsideration (à la zero-based budgeting), and every line of business should be for sale at the right price. In such an experimenting organization, projects wouldn't become institutionalized to the point where management couldn't judge them on their own costs and benefits. And because managers in such a system would be judged as much for recognition of problems facing their units and how they cope with them as for success and failure, experimenting organizations should be extremely flexible. When a market or a technology changes, the experimenting organization would not simply try to patch up the old product or plant but would be quick to see when it is best to pull the plug and start anew.

References

1 For more complete reviews of escalation research, see Barry M. Staw and Jerry Ross, "Understanding Escalation Situations: Antecedents, Prototypes, and Solutions," in *Research in Organizational Behavior*, ed. L.L. Cummings and Barry M. Staw (Greenwich, Conn.: JAI Press, 1987); and Joel Brockner and Jeffrey Z. Rubin, *Entrapment in Escalating Conflicts* (New York: Springer-Verlag, 1985).

2 See Gregory B. Northcraft and Gerrit Wolf, "Dollars, Sense, and Sunk Costs: A Lifecycle Model of Resource Allocation," *Academy of Management Review*, April 1984, p. 22.

3 For experiment results, see Barry M. Staw, "Knee-deep in the Big Muddy: A Study of Escalating Commitment to a Chosen Course of Action," in *Organizational Behavior and Human Performance*, June 1976, p. 27; Alan Tegar, *Too Much Invested to Quit* (New York: Pergamon Press, 1980); and Max H. Bazerman, R.I. Beekum, and F. David Schoorman, "Performance Evaluation in a Dynamic Context: A Laboratory Study of the Impact of Prior Commitment to the Ratee," *Journal of Applied Psychology*, December 1982, p. 873.

4 Frederick V. Fox and Barry M. Staw, "The Trapped Administrator: The Effects of Job Insecurity and Policy Resistance upon Commitment to a Course of Action," *Administrative Science Quarterly*, September 1979, p. 449.

5 Barry M. Staw and Jerry Ross, "Commitment in an Experimenting Society: An Experiment on the Attribution of Leadership from Administrative Scenarios," *Journal of Applied Psychology*, June 1980, p. 249.

6 See Roy J. Lewicki, "Bad Loan Psychology: Entrapment and Commitment in Financial Lending," Graduate School of Business Administration Working Paper No. 80-25 (Durham, N.C.: Duke University, 1980).

7 Bruce E. McCain, "Continuing Investment Under Conditions of Failure: A Laboratory Study of the Limits to Escalation," *Journal of Applied Psychology*, May 1986, p. 280; and Edward G. Conlon and Gerrit Wolf, "The Moderating Effects of Strategy, Visibility, and Involvement on Allocation Behavior: An Extension of Staw's Escalation Paradigm," *Organizational Behavior and Human Performance*, October 1980, p. 172.

8 Donald T. Campbell, "Reforms as Experiments," *American Psychologist*, April 1969, p. 409.

Special Report

Post-project appraisals pay

Frank R. Gulliver

If your company is like most, you spend thousands of hours planning an investment, millions of dollars implementing it – and nothing evaluating and learning from it. As a result, you may not have answers for the most basic questions: Was the investment successful? What made it go according to plan? Did it go according to plan at all? As easy as these questions seem, the answers aren't always obvious.

British Petroleum (BP) built a plant in Australia to convert gas into a component of high-octane gasoline. It came in under budget and ahead of schedule. A similar facility in Rotterdam went over budget and was a year late. BP's managers first drew the obvious conclusion: the Australian plant was a success and the Dutch one a failure. But a second look challenged that first impression.

At the time the Australian project was proposed, that country was suffering from a balance of payments deficit, and the product was expected to help the country reduce its gasoline imports. The plant was completed earlier than expected. But by that time, Australia's economic situation had changed, and gasoline demand turned out to be lower than predicted.

Mr. Gulliver is group internal auditor with the British Petroleum Company. He was a founding member of its post-project appraisal unit, and it remains part of his responsibility today.

Although the Rotterdam project had obvious problems, the market for the product remained strong in Europe. Thus that project's return on investment was in line with predictions, while that of its Australian counterpart was much lower. The Rotterdam project's success taught top managers at BP a valuable lesson: the planners needed to improve their market forecasting techniques.

> *At this moment, managers in every company are making mistakes that no one thinks could be made.*

There is an independent unit at British Petroleum's London headquarters responsible for identifying these kinds of issues – the post-project appraisal unit (PPA). It examines the thinking behind selected investments as well as their management and their results. PPA's sole mission is to help British Petroleum worldwide learn from its mistakes and repeat its successes.

Since its inception at the end of 1977, PPA has appraised more than

80 of BP's worldwide investments, including onshore and offshore construction projects, acquisitions, divestments, project cancellations, research projects, diversification plans, and shipping activities. The appraisals are not academic exercises; the unit seeks to improve company performance.

Through PPA, BP managers have learned how to formulate investment proposals more accurately, approve them more objectively, and execute them more efficiently than ever before. As a result, most projects now generate returns on investment at least as high as those forecast. These improvements have naturally boosted the company's overall financial performance: in 1985, BP's profits reached an all-time high of £1,598 million after taxes. While PPA isn't the only reason for this performance, managers at BP believe the appraisal unit has yielded dramatic results.

Wide-angle inquiry

In talking with businesspeople from large British and multinational corporations, I have found that few companies examine their completed projects in any depth. Most audits are narrowly focused attempts to check that proper controls are in place while a project is in operation. When our managers audit an oil refinery, for example, they gather detailed information about how the oil and gas is collected, measured, shipped, and accounted for.

A post-project appraisal, however, takes a much larger view. It first looks at the big questions: Why was the project started in the first place? Is it producing as much oil as the proposal predicted? Is the demand for oil at the forecasted level? Did the contractors deliver what they promised? Does the project fit well into BP's overall corporate strategy?

In "post-completion reviews," some U.S. corporations attempt a similar sort of wide-angle evaluation of past projects. But these differ from BP's post-project appraisals in two ways: objectivity and applicability. Because project members usually conduct post-completion reviews, they are more likely to have preconceived ideas or even a vested interest in the reviews' outcomes. The members of BP's PPA unit have no affiliation with the projects they appraise and so can evaluate investments more objectively.

Moreover, post-completion reviews usually don't guarantee that the lessons will reach the people who need them most, because the information spreads by word of mouth. PPA, in contrast, is a centralized department that can inspect any type of investment in any part of the far-flung BP group and transmit information from one site to another. It can learn lessons from an oil refinery project in France and teach them to planners working on a similar plant in Australia.

PPA is also part of BP's investment proposal procedure. The unit reviews all new investment proposals to make sure that no one repeats mistakes. When they have time, unit members will even work with project planners to formulate proposals.

Appraisal operations

The PPA unit consists of a manager and four assistants, reporting directly to BP's board of directors. In the unit's nine-year history, the composition of the staff has, of course, changed a few times. PPA managers, however, have to meet the same criteria: they must be acceptable to the most senior echelons of management and must have at least 15 years of broad-based experience at BP. The company chooses the other staff members for their specific expertise. They might be engineers, chemists, physicists, economists, or accountants. A team of two or three unit members investigates each project.

An appraisal of a large investment generally takes about six months to complete. Because the company can absorb only so much information at a time, the unit limits its major appraisals to six per year. The most valuable lessons come from the largest projects, where BP stands to lose or gain the most money. PPA selects its projects carefully, looking for those that will yield the most valuable results.

The unit does not therefore investigate a project if its lessons will duplicate those drawn from a previous appraisal. Nor does it evaluate a project

that BP is unlikely to do again. The unit once considered appraising a large crude-oil sale contract that BP had made with another big oil company. Because the Middle Eastern nations had nationalized their oil fields, however, BP no longer made such sales. The unit consequently decided not to study the project.

Getting started. BP is divided into 11 businesses, each with its own board of directors and chief executive. These businesses report to BP's central management, which is headed by the main board of directors. A corporate review committee of BP's main board must approve each PPA appraisal. This committee both oversees the unit's activities and examines all proposed capital investments for compatibility with BP's corporate strategy. PPA submits proposals for projects it could appraise in 18 months to two years, and the committee generally accepts them, though it occasionally adds or deletes one or two.

The unit staff then determines the order in which to carry out the appraisals and, with the chief executive of the project's business, sets a broad timetable for each investigation.

A PPA team examines a project from its conception – before the proposal is even written – usually until two years after it has become operational. The team tries to determine systematically how a project was handled: at the proposal stage; during the project's construction (or, in the case of an acquisition, during the target company's purchase); during the project's operation (or the acquired company's integration into BP); and during the post-operation (or post-integration) stage. PPA always tries to determine the important factors that contribute to a project's problems or success.

Although it usually learns more by seeing how problems developed, the unit also finds it useful to pinpoint the causes of success. The purchase of a Dutch nutrition company called Hendrix, top management agreed, was one of the smoothest acquisitions ever. PPA ascribed its success largely to the precision with which the planners had determined the extent of Hendrix's integration into BP.

Files and interviews. At an appraisal's outset, the team relies on

the files to become familiar with the project. This avoids wasting people's time. The team learns about the economic climate at the time, the identity of the contractors, or the chemical process used. Team members might spend the first two months of a six-month investigation just looking at files – both at project files and at material in related corporate files, in such departments as accounting, legal, or planning.

While the PPA manager will probably already know the senior managers who should be interviewed, the files provide a complete list. The team generally tries to interview everyone involved in the project. Since most projects have been completed for at least two years before the unit begins its work, however, the project members are working all over the world on other things. In one investigation, the PPA team talked to 80 individuals; the average is usually around 40.

In their interviews, the PPA team members make an effort to understand the psychology of the project members and managers. They interview in pairs so that one team member can ask questions while the other watches the interviewee. A furtive look often tells as much as a direct answer.

After the interview, the two team members compare notes and reconcile differences in their perceptions. The full story usually emerges in separate pieces: senior managers in London will give up one piece of information; engineers on an oil rig in the middle of the North Sea will give up another. By melding project members' different perspectives, the PPA people can come up with the whole picture.

PPA team members realize that project employees shed light on is-

Four lessons

Over the past ten years, PPA has taught BP management four main lessons. These are:

Determine costs accurately
Before PPA existed, BP's management approved unrealistically low budgets because planners inaccurately predicted the scope of the project when they submitted the budget. Now BP approves budgets in phases, and each phase becomes more accurate as planners work out the project's details.

In the first phase, the engineers offer an approximate figure for the project's budget that could be off by as much as 50%. The board then approves about 1% of this sum to pay outside engineers and consultants to develop the case more fully. The engineers then submit a more accurate budget. Eventually, at the time the board approves the entire project, it adopts a final budget, which should be off by no more than 10%.

BP now pays more attention to the technical requirements of local health, safety, and environmental legislation. Company managers look beyond simply what the legislation requires; to estimate costs accurately, BP planners solve any design problems created by such regulations in the proposal stage.

Managers now are careful not to rush a project's approval so it can qualify for a government grant or other bonus. A rushed project is often inadequately defined and therefore out of control from the start, runs very late, and comes in over budget—so much over budget that costs substantially exceed the incentive.

The corporation no longer automatically awards a contract to the lowest bidder. Many low bids come in because contractors don't fully understand what BP needs. PPA has found a correlation between low bids and poor contractor performance.

Anticipate and minimize risk
Fearing that a competitor would snatch the opportunity, BP businesses wishing to acquire another company would often try to speed up the examination and the decision-making process. According to the PPA unit, such self-imposed deadlines are usually illusory. Moreover, the unit has found that if the company is not satisfied about the soundness of an acquisition proposal, BP will probably not regret the missed opportunity.

BP used to expand plant capacity without knowing whether it could sell all of the product the new plant could then produce. Now before adding capacity or introducing a product, the company requires planners to submit a full market survey to verify that a market will exist and be profitable.

Evaluate contractors
BP now has a contractor evaluation unit that monitors potential contractors' performance. When it solicits bids, the corporation already knows which contractor would be most likely to perform to its satisfaction. Formerly, BP used an unsophisticated method to select contractors. It was ignorant of contractors' deficiencies and performance for other companies in different parts of the world.

To make certain that a contractor has expertise in a project's process technology, BP now pays careful attention to the caliber of the contractor's key staff members and insists that they remain with the project to the end.

Improve project management
Engineers do not automatically make good managers. The company frequently used to send an engineer from a project in one part of the world to one halfway around the world. No one asked whether the engineer was familiar with the project, the country, or even the main contractor. At the recommendation of PPA, BP set up a projects department that helps engineers develop appropriate control techniques and procedures and ensures that the right person manages the right project.

To make project progress reports more constructive, the projects department has set up a projects control division. This division uses software programs, linked to each project, to help the project manager issue reports that identify likely problems and give reasons for missed milestones. These reports can be fed through the project control division's computer center for evaluation on a day-by-day, or even a minute-by-minute, basis.

The projects department ensures that project managers are appointed early enough to involve them with the design considerations, project strategies, and control mechanisms. With the projects department's guidance, project managers can make more independent decisions.

Capital investment analysts have usually swamped managers with advice based on well-meaning academic research, but it has been limited to questions about acquisition. Now, through post-project appraisal, managers can get sound advice on questions about many kinds of projects from the experience of their own companies.

sues that may seem unrelated to their areas of expertise. Those working out in the field often live together, eat together, and go out drinking together. Not surprisingly, an accountant may offer a cogent insight about the head engineer, even though they did not actually work closely with each other.

Sending PPA teams into the field to conduct investigations is far more expensive than sending out questionnaires—and far more effective. Because a questionnaire is a set collection of questions, it can elicit only a limited view of the project. In an interview, people offer unexpected information;

also, the PPA team can lead an interviewee away from digressions.

Conclusions and reactions.
The post-project appraisal unit has had very little trouble getting cooperation from BP's staff. In the unit's nine-year life, the PPA teams have found that people genuinely want to help the company grow more profitable by joining in an examination of performance. Even individuals who have been singled out for blame continue to see the unit's value. In one case, an appraisal concluded that a senior manager had not done his job

well. The corporate review committee called him in and raked him over the coals. For some time, relations between the manager and the PPA unit were cool. But a few months later, he telephoned the PPA manager to ask if the unit had appraised any projects similar to one he was beginning. He wanted advice.

The staff cooperates with the unit partly because it gives them a chance to take issue with conclusions before they appear in PPA's report. It is a testament to the fairness and accuracy of the unit's work that no one has ever taken advantage of this opportunity.

After the team has exhausted the files, interviewed everyone involved, and digested and assembled the information in a preliminary draft to circulate to key managers, it submits a final draft to the business board and then to the corporate review committee.

> *The most valuable lessons come from the biggest projects, where the most money is at stake.*

The committee carefully considers PPA's work and almost always supports the conclusions: it has received many hundreds of recommendations and has rejected only one. This suggestion—that BP maintain a staff of experts in different metallurgical technologies to supplement contractors—was simply too expensive.

BP does not circulate throughout the corporation the full reports on each appraisal, although these do go to relevant managers, but collates them into three booklets—one on acquisitions, another on joint ventures, and the last on project development and control. PPA regularly updates these booklets—adding lessons learned from later appraisals and occasionally deleting a lesson that no longer applies. One was a recommendation to build refinery plants on the Continent rather than in Britain because of poor labor relations in the United Kingdom. But labor relations have improved greatly since then.

BP's upper management expects project planners to use the information in the booklets as guidelines when writing proposals. A proposal that does not meet all the guidelines should not necessarily be abandoned. But if planners cannot comply with the guidelines, the corporate review committee will want to see that the proposal accounts for the possible risks.

PPA sends the booklets to the London headquarters of each of BP's 11 businesses and to each of the approximately 30 major BP associate companies worldwide. If any section of the corporation needs more copies, the unit willingly sends them along. The PPA philosophy is that the company's investment performance will only improve as more BP people learn what went wrong and what went right in the past.

From its experimental and tentative beginnings a decade ago, PPA has grown into an integral part of BP's planning and control process. It succeeds because of its consistent reputation for digging out the truth. The unit enjoys the full confidence of BP's senior managers and directors because they believe that both the facts and the conclusions in the reports are accurate. This accuracy is based on the investigating team's thoroughness, its understanding of the technical issues, its fairness in evaluating the evidence, and its sensitivity to the psychological forces motivating the staff. In that accuracy lies the usefulness of the lessons to the corporation and the success of the post-project appraisal unit.

Appraisal lessons

There is a big difference between classroom lessons about business and lessons drawn from experience. What might seem self-evident or unlikely in theory may be the most important factor in an actual event. To illustrate, let me describe a project from a time before BP implemented many of the procedures PPA recommended.

In 1967, a director at BP responsible for engineering and refining wanted to explore a technology that Exxon and others were using but that was new to BP. The man was well respected within the company and had a great deal of influence. By the force of his personality, he pushed through a proposal for the construction of the biggest plant of its kind that BP had ever built. Exxon had a plant that turned out 30,000 barrels of oil per day on three production lines; the BP installation would produce that volume on a single line. This line required the largest compressors and pumps that BP had ever used and completely new technology in the reactor vessels.

During construction and testing, the company had difficulty with all three. It had particular trouble with the reactor vessels, which, because of their size, had to be thinner than conventional vessels and thus needed lining with stainless steel. Despite assurances to management that the job was easy, BP's contractor ran into one problem after another. Finally, BP's own engineers solved the problems at great expense.

BP learned much from PPA's investigation of this experience. It learned that it must assess proposals more carefully. It learned to assess a new technology's risks more thoroughly and more objectively. It learned that it had to improve its method of selecting contractors. Perhaps the company should have learned these lessons already. But obviously it had not—and the post-project appraisal process brought them to light, formalized them, and collected them in one place.

Managers in every company are making mistakes no one thinks could be made. Time after time, the post-project appraisal unit has uncovered these kinds of mistakes and helped British Petroleum avoid repeating them.

READ THE FINE PRINT

REPRINTS
Telephone: 617-495-6192
Fax: 617-495-6985

Current and past articles are available, as is an annually updated index. Discounts apply to large-quantity purchases.

Please send orders to HBR Reprints, Harvard Business School Publishing Division, Boston, MA 02163.

HOW CAN *HARVARD BUSINESS REVIEW* ARTICLES WORK FOR YOU?

For years, we've printed a microscopically small notice on the editorial credits page of the *Harvard Business Review* alerting our readers to the availability of *HBR* articles.

Now we invite you to take a closer look at how you can put this hard-working business tool to work for you.

IN THE CORPORATE CLASSROOM

There's no more effective, or cost-effective, way to supplement your corporate training programs than in-depth, incisive *HBR* articles.

At just $3.50 a copy—even less for quantity orders—it's no wonder hundreds of companies use *HBR* articles for management training.

IN-BOX INNOVATION

Where do your company's movers and shakers get their big ideas? Many find inspiration in the pages of *HBR*. They then share the wealth by distributing *HBR* articles to colleagues.

IN MARKETING AND SALES SUPPORT

HBR articles are a substantive leave-behind to your sales calls. They add credibility to your direct mail campaigns. And demonstrate that your company is on the leading edge of business thinking.

CREATE CUSTOM ARTICLES

If you want even greater impact, personalize *HBR* articles with your company's name or logo. And put your name in front of your customers.

DISCOVER MORE REASONS IN THE *HBR CATALOG*.

In all, the *Harvard Business Review Catalog* lists articles on over 500 different subjects. Plus, you'll find collections, books, and videos on subjects you need to know. The catalog is yours for just $10.00. Order today. And start putting *HBR* articles to work for you.

How To Order. To order individual articles or the *HBR Catalog*, dial toll-free in the continental U.S. 1-800-545-7685. Outside the U.S. call 617-495-6192. **Please mention telephone code 165A** when placing your order. Or FAX your order to 617-495-6985. You may also send a check payable to Harvard Business School Publishing Division, or credit card information to: HBR Articles, Harvard Business School Publishing Division, Operations Department, Boston, MA 02163. **All orders must be prepaid.**

Order No.	Title	Qty. X	Price +	Shipping =	Total
21018	Catalog		$10		

U.S. and Canada: 5% for UPS or first class mail. *Foreign Surface Mail:* 15% for parcel post registered; allow 3–6 mos. *Express Deliveries (credit card orders only):* billed at cost; all foreign orders not designating express delivery will be sent by registered surface mail.

☐ Check enclosed (in U.S. funds drawn on U.S. bank)

☐ VISA   ☐ American Express   ☐ MasterCard

Card Number_____ Exp. Date_____

Signature_____

Telephone_____FAX_____

Name_____

Organization_____

Street_____

City_____

State/Zip_____

Country_____

Harvard Business School Publishing

☐ Home address   ☐ Organization address

PLEASE REFERENCE TELEPHONE ORDER SOURCE CODE 165A

• SPECIAL COLLECTIONS • BOOKS • HBR ARTICLES • CUSTOM HBR ARTICLES • VIDEOS • CASES •

YOU SAID: AND WE SAID:

"Give us training tools that are relevant to our business...ones we can use *now*."

"We need new cases that stimulate meaningful discussion."

"It can't be a catalog of canned programs... everything we do is custom."

"Make it a single source for up-to-date materials ...on the most current business topics."

"Better yet if it's from a reputable business school. That adds credibility."

Harvard Business School Publishing

"Introducing the Harvard Business School Corporate Training and Development Catalog."

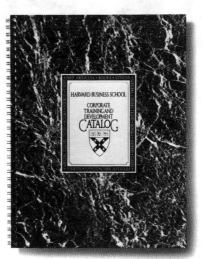

You asked for it. And now it's here.

The new Harvard Business School Corporate Training and Development Catalog is created exclusively for those who design and develop custom training programs.

It's filled cover-to-cover with valuable materials you can put to work on the spot. You'll find a comprehensive selection of cases, *Harvard Business Review* articles, videos, Special Collections, books, and more.

Our new catalog covers the critical management topics affecting corporations today, like Leadership, Quality, Global Business, Marketing, and Strategy, to name a few. And it's all organized, indexed, and cross-referenced to make it easy for you to find precisely what you need.

HOW TO ORDER

To order by FAX, dial 617-495-6985. Or call 617-495-6192. Please mention telephone order code 132A. Or send a check for $10 payable to HBS Publishing Division, or credit card information to: HBS Corporate Training and Development Catalog, Harvard Business School Publishing Division, Operations Department, Boston, MA 02163. **All orders must be prepaid.**

Order No.	Title	Qty. ×	Price +	Shipping* =	Total
39001	Catalog		$10		

*U.S. and Canada: 5% for UPS or first class mail. *Foreign Surface Mail:* 15% for parcel post registered; allow 3-6 mos. *Express Deliveries (credit card orders only):* billed at cost; all foreign orders not designating express delivery will be sent by registered surface mail.

☐ Check enclosed (in U.S. funds drawn on U.S. bank)

☐ VISA ☐ American Express ☐ MasterCard

Card Number_____ Exp. Date_____

Signature_____

Telephone_____ FAX_____

Name_____

Organization_____

Street_____

City_____ State/Zip_____

Country_____ ☐ Home Address ☐ Organization Address

Please Reference Telephone Order Source Code 132A

• SPECIAL COLLECTIONS • BOOKS • HBR ARTICLES • CUSTOM HBR ARTICLES • VIDEOS • CASES •